Studies in the general
Epistles of John

Tests of Life

by **Theodore H. Epp**
Director
Back to the Bible Broadcast

A
BACK TO THE BIBLE
PUBLICATION

Back to the Bible
Lincoln, Nebraska 68501

140,000 printed to date—1981
(5-0416—70M—81)
ISBN 0-8474-0450-1

Printed in the United States of America

Foreword

Counterfeit Christianity cannot stand before the test of life outlined in the Book of I John. Empty profession stands indicted like the Church of Laodicea: "Thou art wretched, and miserable, and poor, and blind, and naked" (Rev. 3:17).

On the other hand, there is both comfort and challenge for the true believer in Christ in this brief epistle. The comfort is in the evidences of eternal life by which the Christian can test his own experience. The challenge lies in the high standards of conduct God sets for His children. We must remember that every challenge of this type in the Word of God carries with it God's power for accomplishment.

Mr. Epp has also drawn practical lessons for our day from II and III John.

This material on the General Epistles of John has been adapted from a series of radio messages given by Mr. Epp over the Back to the Bible Broadcast.

Bible students have long recognized that John's epistles contain some passages that are hard to understand. These portions have been given special attention by Mr. Epp, and we believe his treatment of them is scriptural.

—The Publishers

Contents

Introduction

The writer of these epistles, who was dear to the heart of Jesus and known as the beloved disciple, also wrote the Gospel of John and the Book of the Revelation.

Comparing the Gospel With the Epistle

There are a number of points of similarity and contrast between the Gospel of John and I John. In the Gospel he said, "These are written, that ye might believe that Jesus is the Christ, the Son of God; and that believing ye might have life through his name" (John 20:31). In his first epistle he said, "These things have I written unto you that believe on the name of the Son of God; that ye may know that ye have eternal life, and that ye may believe on the name of the Son of God" (I John 5:13). In both of these passages Jesus Christ is described as the Son of God, but the reasons for presenting His deity differ. In the Gospel of John, Jesus Christ is presented as the source and means of eternal life through faith, and the message is therefore directed to unbelievers. First John, on the other hand, is addressed to believers—those persons who have accepted the Son of God as their Saviour and thereby have assurance of their possession of eternal life.

This epistle was written so that believers might

know that they have eternal life. Believers bring no glory to God if they doubt His Word. Without this assurance they are useless in their service to God. How can they effectively point others to Christ as Saviour if they are not certain about their own salvation?

Assurance of salvation does not give us license to sin. The whole emphasis of this short epistle refutes that conclusion. This book deals with fellowship with Christ and with God the Father. Unless we have assurance of salvation, how can we have any fellowship? The whole walk with Christ is based on the knowledge of whether or not we have trusted Jesus as Saviour.

Some people say they will never know whether or not they are saved until they get to heaven and God tests all their works. God's Word does not support this idea. We should know the difference between the salvation provided for us by God and the work He does through us once we are saved. Assurance of salvation is not only a possibility but a necessity if we are to provide the best kind of service for the Lord.

In John's Gospel eternal life is unveiled and manifested in Christ the Son. There we learn what eternal life is and how we may receive it. In I John, on the other hand, we learn that eternal life is the possession of the children of God and is manifested to the world through them.

Evidences of Life

In the Gospel of John we learn that the Lord Jesus came to dwell among us. He was the eternal Word made flesh, He manifested the glory of the

Father, and He was full of grace and truth (1:14). In I John, grace and truth are seen in the lives of believers because Christ indwells them. From this we learn how a Christian should act, and, in addition, these evidences of the Christian life become tests whereby we can know whether or not we have eternal life. John tells us that the Christ-life within the believer will express itself in a certain way, and this in turn becomes a means of identifying the true believer.

Other portions of the Bible teach this same truth. For instance, James said, "What doth it profit, my brethren, though a man say he hath faith, and have not works? Can faith save him?" (James 2:14). He was saying, "Is the faith that does not result in good works the kind of faith that saves?" Then he goes on to show that the person who has saving faith will exhibit it in the kind of life he lives.

Paul, in writing to the Ephesians, stated the same truth. Sometimes we quote Ephesians 2:8,9 but fail to recognize what verse 10 says. "For by grace are ye saved through faith; and that not of yourselves: it is the gift of God: not of works, lest any man should boast. For we are his workmanship, created in Christ Jesus unto good works." So in this way, we confess our faith. The whole epistle of I John is built around this idea. We can know for certain by examining our conduct whether or not our faith is genuine.

My own experience illustrates this. At the age of 15 I studied a catechism. I memorized it. I could answer the questions. The final questions, which related to salvation, I also answered correctly, as a preacher's son should. Then I was baptized and

9

joined a church. It was not until about five years later that I realized I had not received Christ into my heart. I knew the creed, but I wasn't saved. Five years elapsed from the time I was baptized and joined the church until I realized my need of Christ as Saviour and received Him as such. At that time I experienced a change of heart and began to have desires that I John says should follow genuine salvation.

These same tests also serve to show believers if they are growing in the Christian life. This will become clearer as the study progresses. It is a very important matter. Wherever we test for evidence of new life in Christ, we can also test for evidence of growth toward maturity in that life.

Three Key Words

There are three key words in the epistle of I John. They are life, light and love. These words are used many times in this epistle.

That God has given us eternal life is clearly stated in I John 5:11-13, which are key verses to the study of this epistle. God has given us eternal life, and that life is in His Son. If we have the Son, we have eternal life; if we do not have the Son, we do not have eternal life.

Eternal life is a special quality of life which makes it possible for us to fellowship with God. More than eternal duration of life is meant. The unsaved exist eternally, but nowhere does the Bible describe their experience as eternal life. Existence apart from God, even though people are able to think, speak, feel and remember, is not life but death. Christ Jesus is the source of eternal life.

Indeed, He is the believer's eternal life, and His character is that of life. This will become more evident.

Some may wonder how they can have the Son and have life. John's Gospel makes this plain: "He came unto his own, and his own received him not. But as many as received him, to them gave he power to become the sons of God, even to them that believe on his name: which were born, not of blood, nor of the will of the flesh, nor of the will of man, but of God" (1:11-13).

The other two words, light and love, provide the test whereby we may know whether or not that life is within us. We are told that God, as to His nature, is light and that there is no darkness in Him. And if we walk in the light as He is in the light, we have fellowship one with the other. Light reveals righteousness, and it also reveals sin. By virtue of the light, we can know whether or not we have eternal life.

The love spoken of is a God-given love, and it becomes both the outward expression of the inward life and another test whereby we may know that we have such life. The love of God has been shed abroad in our hearts by the Holy Spirit (Rom. 5:5) so that the man who is born of God loves others. This is the very essence of Christianity.

Chapter 1

Fellowship Made Possible Through Christ

"That which was from the beginning, which we have heard, which we have seen with our eyes, which we have looked upon, and our hands have handled, of the Word of life; (for the life was manifested, and we have seen it, and bear witness, and shew unto you that eternal life, which was with the Father, and was manifested unto us;) that which we have seen and heard declare we unto you, that ye also may have fellowship with us: and truly our fellowship is with the Father, and with his Son Jesus Christ. And these things write we unto you, that your joy may be full" (I John 1:1-4).

It is not possible for us in our natural life to have fellowship with God. We cannot fellowship with God unless we have God's life. This was made possible through Christ, who is the eternal Son and who entered into a human body, was born of the virgin Mary, dwelt among men and suffered and died on Calvary to provide eternal salvation for us. This is what John referred to when he wrote of the one who was from the beginning and whom the disciples had heard and seen and handled.

Through doing this Christ made eternal life accessible to us. How much in common this has with John's Gospel is shown by John 1:1,2: "In the beginning was the Word, and the Word was with God, and the Word was God. The same was in the beginning with God." In verse 14 of the same chapter we read: "And the Word was made flesh, and dwelt among us, (and we beheld his glory, the glory as of the only begotten of the Father,) full of grace and truth."

Proofs of the Incarnation

The Apostle John was seeking to offset a heresy which was prevalent in his day—that Jesus Christ did not come in the flesh. To refute this heresy he emphasized four things with reference to the incarnation. First, he called on the evidence of the ears—he said, "We have heard" (I John 1:1). John and the other apostles heard the voice of the Son of God, for He walked among them for some three and one-half years. They listened to His instructions and admonitions.

They not only heard Him, but they also saw Him, for John said, "We have seen with our eyes" (v. 1). But they did more than see Him; they "looked upon" (v. 1), or closely observed, Him. This suggests study and personal investigation, not just a look.

Several years ago it was my privilege to be in Washington, D. C., and along with some 800 other people I had breakfast with some of our political leaders. The vice-president of our country was there. I saw him eat, and I sometimes teasingly say that I had breakfast with him, even though I was not at the same table. I saw him, but I did not observe him closely. On the other hand, I have worked with some people for years here at Back to the Bible. I have closely observed them. I know their hearts' desires. There is a world of difference

14

between merely seeing someone and really observing someone.

The fourth thing John said was "Our hands have handled, of the Word of life" (v. 1). John used the sense of touch as proof of the reality of the incarnation of Christ.

When Thomas questioned the resurrection of the Lord, our Saviour appeared before him and said, "Reach hither thy finger, and behold my hands; and reach hither thy hand, and thrust it into my side: and be not faithless, but believing" (John 20:27). No wonder Thomas said, "My Lord and my God" (v. 28).

John said that the One who existed from all eternity, the Creator of life Himself, is the One who came in the flesh. He came to give us eternal life. We already had created life from Him. But eternal life is not ordinary life. It is not only eternal in its length of existence, but it is of a different quality than any other life. It is a particular kind of life. This life makes it possible for us to fellowship with God.

In I John 1:2 John said, "We . . . bear witness, and shew unto you that eternal life." What is a witness? According to verse 1, it is one who saw, heard, looked upon and handled, or touched, the living Christ. The witness of the apostles was actually twofold. First, they told of their experience. Then they showed by their behavior that they had new life within them. We cannot say that we have seen the physical form of our Lord, but like the apostles, we have received Him as Saviour, and He now lives His life through us. Of course, we, too, can witness by word of mouth; however, we are

15

not only to talk about Christianity but also to live it.

The next idea we want to consider is fellowship. We cannot fellowship with something abstract; it can be done only with a person. That person must be someone who has something in common with us. We cannot have fellowship with God without having God's life. Fellowship has been defined as a joint participation with someone else in things held in common by both. This means that those who have fellowship with Jesus must participate in things they have in common with Him. For instance, we must participate in His life. "He that hath the Son hath life; and he that hath not the Son of God hath not life" (5:12). We must also have His nature, which is the result of that life. From that will flow His love, a love that will seek righteousness and hate sin. If we want to fellowship with Jesus, we must seek to do the will of the Father as He did it.

This same eternal life is in all believers. We are all members of His Body. Physically speaking, I have only one life which flows through my entire body. The life in my hand is not different from the life in my foot. And so, as members of the Body of Christ, Christians have the same life and can fellowship together.

Testing the Life by Light

First John 1:5 says, "That God is light, and in him is no darkness at all." John did not say that God is *a* light, nor did he say that God is *the* light. As to His nature, God *is* light. He is not like an

16

electric light which can be turned off and on, but rather He is like the electricity itself.

Light is perfectly pure and is incapable of pollution. In the Scripture it is used as a symbol for infinite holiness, infinite purity and perfect righteousness.

Light also makes sight possible, and God, who is light, has infinite knowledge. Nothing in creation is hidden from Him. No transaction takes place that is not seen by Him. The adulterer, the thief and the murderer are all known to Him. He not only sees our ways, but He also sees our very hearts. He knows the thoughts of our minds. He knows our attitudes and our motives. There is no darkness in Him at all. Nothing is concealed from His eyes.

We may think, because we see so much sin around us, that God does not really rule the earth, but He does. God is light. Darkness may be all around Him, but it is not in Him. There is not a shade of sin in God. Sin and darkness cannot exist in Him. There can be no mixture of good and evil in Him. There can be no ignorance or deceit with Him, for He is God and He is light.

Since there is no union between light and darkness, there remains a separation between us and God as long as we walk in darkness. There is no ground for fellowship under such conditions. "The light shineth in darkness; and the darkness comprehended [overpowered] it not" (John 1:5). In the struggle between light and darkness, light was victorious—Christ was victorious.

God is omniscient. He is all-wise. There is no ignorance with Him. The psalmist declared, "O Lord, thou hast searched me, and known me. Thou

17

knowest my downsitting and mine uprising, thou understandest my thought afar off" (Ps. 139:1,2). This is encouraging for persons walking in the light, but to those who are not, the next few verses may cause apprehension: "Thou compassest my path and my lying down, and art acquainted with all my ways. For there is not a word in my tongue, but, lo, O Lord, thou knowest it altogether. Thou hast beset me behind and before, and laid thine hand upon me. Such knowledge is too wonderful for me; it is high, I cannot attain unto it" (vv. 3-6).

The psalmist also realized that he could hide nothing from God, for he continued: "If I say, Surely the darkness shall cover me; even the night shall be light about me. Yea, the darkness hideth not from thee; but the night shineth as the day: the darkness and the light are both alike to thee" (vv. 11,12).

God revealed Himself as light through His Son. Christ was the light who shined in the darkness. He revealed the absolute holiness and purity of God. He also revealed the love of God for us. He taught us what sin and its awful consequences were, and He declared that no one who has ignored their own sin and the Son of God can stand in God's presence.

Three Groups of Religious Sinners

Three groups of religious sinners are exposed in the last part of I John 1. Perhaps some of these have eternal life and are ignorant concerning sin. But we must remember that the light of God exposes all hypocrisy in believers, and there would be no rest in their hearts until sin is dealt with. The first group of sinners think they are God's children, but they continue to practice sin, which only proves that they either are ignorant of God's way of salvation or are ignorant of the quality of life that God gives believers.

The second group, described in verse 8, claim Christianity but deny having the depraved nature. Such people might be unsaved or saved, for there are believers who say their old natures have been eradicated. The verdict of God is that they are deceiving themselves; they do not deceive anybody else.

The third group is mentioned in verse 10: "If we say that we have not sinned, we make him a liar, and his word is not in us." These people deny that they have committed sins.

Notice what these different groups claim to have, and compare their conduct with their claims. Then notice what God says concerning their condemnation and what cure God has provided for each group.

First Group of Religious Sinners

The first religious group claims to have fellowship with God, but they continue to walk in darkness (I John 1:6). Their conduct disproves their claim. They also claim, of course, to have eternal life, to be joint-heirs with Christ, to live godly lives and to have likes and dislikes in common with those who have new life in Christ. But they walk in darkness.

It is important to note that John often used what is known as the present indicative tense, which in the Greek language indicates a good deal more than something taking place in present time. The emphasis is not on the time element so much

19

as on the action of the verb. In the present tense, the action is continued, or habitual, action. So I John 1:6 could be translated: "If we habitually, or continually, walk in darkness and claim to have fellowship with Christ, we are lying."

How similar this sounds to the message that was given to the Church of Sardis: "And unto the angel of the church in Sardis write; These things saith he that hath the seven Spirits of God, and the seven stars; I know thy works, that thou hast a name that thou livest, and art dead" (Rev. 3:1). The ever-present danger in our churches today is that we may drift into a dead orthodoxy. Apparently this is what happened in Sardis, and this is what John was warning about.

Many today trust in a name or in conformity to external practices and have never known the peace and purity which Christ gives. "If any man be in Christ, he is a new creature: old things are passed away" (II Cor. 5:17).

A Twofold Cure

The cure for those in this group is twofold. First John 1:7 says, "But if we walk in the light, as he is in the light, we have fellowship one with another, and the blood of Jesus Christ his Son cleanseth us from all sin." The first part of the cure is to walk in the light. The verse does not say to walk according to the light. Where we walk determines how we walk; therefore, we should walk in the light. "All things . . . are made manifest by the light" (Eph. 5:13), and to walk in the light is to walk in the presence of God. That in itself will bring consciousness of any sin in our lives.

For a person to walk in the light requires that he first receive Christ as personal Saviour. The light of God's Word must first have enlightened that person's heart and convicted him of his sin. That same light reveals to us the holiness of God and brings us to a reverential fear of Him, something foreign to the natural man (see Rom. 3:18).

That same light reveals to us how Christ came to reconcile us to God. To us is offered "the righteousness of God which is by faith of Jesus Christ unto all and upon all them that believe: for there is no difference" (v. 22).

An admonition is stated in Colossians 2:6: "As ye have therefore received Christ Jesus the Lord, so walk ye in him." Notice that the walking is not according to Him but in Him. Walking in the light, then, is possible only through faith in Christ.

The second cure is cleansing by the blood. The Scriptures tell us that without the shedding of blood there is no remission, or forgiveness, of sin (see Heb. 9:22).

Two aspects of salvation are included in the shed blood of Christ. In Romans 3:25 we read: "Whom God hath set forth to be a propitiation through faith in his blood, to declare his righteousness for the remission of sins that are past, through the forbearance of God." This deals with the shedding of His blood for our justification. Through this we are cleansed from the guilt, judgment and condemnation of sin.

There is a second aspect, however, to the cleansing power of the blood. "The blood of Jesus Christ his Son cleanseth us from all sin" (I John 1:7). This relates to our sanctification and deals

21

with cleansing from the dominion and power of sin. Here the present tense, the tense of continuous action, is used again. So the verse conveys the idea that the blood keeps on cleansing us from all sin.

Justification is not the only thing involved in salvation. Through justification we are acquitted from the guilt and condemnation of sin and at the same time given a place of righteousness before God in Christ. But this is not all there is to the great work of redemption.

At the same time that we were justified, we were given the Holy Spirit, who sealed us. This sealing is described as the "earnest of our inheritance until the redemption of the purchased possession, unto the praise of his glory" (Eph. 1:14). We are now waiting for the redemption of our bodies according to Romans 8:23. Our being sealed by the Holy Spirit is God's assurance that He will complete the work of redemption, and when the body is redeemed, the consummation of salvation will have been reached.

As already noted, justification pronounces us righteous in God's sight and acquits us of the guilt of sin and of sin's condemnation. Sanctification, however, has to do with cleansing from the power and dominion of sin in our present life, and it is in this respect that the blood of Jesus Christ continuously cleanses us from all sin.

As we walk in the light, the blood continuously cleanses us from sins of omission, sins of commission, sins of thought and all the works that the flesh would produce in us. Our old sin nature is not eradicated, but we can have victory over it. Through the Holy Spirit, God enlightens us, and

then by the blood of Jesus Christ we are continuously cleansed if we walk in the light. God says,
in effect, "I will see to it that you will not fulfill
the lusts of the flesh" (Gal. 5:16).

Second Group of Religious Sinners

The second type of religious sinner is described
in I John 1:8: "If we say that we have no sin, we
deceive ourselves, and the truth is not in us." Some
claim to have reached an advanced stage of Christian experience so that they have no sinful nature.

Christians who walk in the light become increasingly conscious of the holiness of God and of
the sinfulness of sin. They are not deluded into
denying that they have a sinful nature. They realize
that they still have sinful tendencies which are expressed in fleshly impulses, nonspiritual inclina-
tions and standards of living that are patterned
after the world rather than after God. These are all
sinful in the sight of God, and to call them righteous rather than sinful is to walk in darkness.
Should we even so much as waver in our trust in
God, we sin, for the Word says, "Whatsoever is not
of faith is sin" (Rom. 14:23).

God says that those who claim to have no sinful nature deceive themselves. They lead themselves astray. God is never deceived by these pre-
tenses and very few human beings are either.

These people are deceived with their own
pride, and the truth is not in them. The presence of
Jesus in the heart increases the believer's sense of
the holiness of God, and he becomes increasingly
more sensitive in detecting sin.

What is the cure for this type of religious sinner? The answer is stated in I John 1:9: "If we confess our sins, he is faithful and just to forgive us our sins, and to cleanse us from all unrighteousness." The word "confess" means "to agree with." It means to say the same thing that God says about our sin. If you have been guilty of this sin, will you confess it to God? He will forgive you. Believe Him and trust Him, and He will cleanse you. The Prodigal Son said, "I will arise and go to my father" (Luke 15:18). Will you?

Third Group of Religious Sinners

The third type of religious sinner is described in I John 1:10: "If we say that we have not sinned, we make him a liar, and his word is not in us." Sin has been revealed to these people. Light has shown in their hearts, but they refuse to acknowledge the sin disclosed. Surely this is depravity in the extreme and could be possible only of an unsaved person.

There are several good illustrations in the Scriptures of this type of sinner. Two of these are found in Luke 18. The first example is in the parable of the Pharisee and the publican. These two men went to the temple to pray. The Pharisee stood and prayed, "God, I thank thee, that I am not as other men are, extortioners, unjust, adulterers, or even as this publican. I fast twice in the week, I give tithes of all that I possess" (vv. 11,12). This man did not once admit that he had committed sinful acts. He boasted before God of the religious things he had done and contrasted himself with the publican.

In that same chapter in Luke is the story of the rich young ruler who wanted to know what he should do to inherit eternal life. He claimed to have kept all the commandments from the time of his youth. But the Saviour stripped all the hypocrisy from his claims by telling him to sell all his property and use the money to feed the poor. He was promised treasure in heaven for so doing. Then he was to follow the Saviour. Instead of this, the ruler went away sorrowful, for he had many possessions. He was very rich, and his wealth came before God. Like the Pharisee, he was saying, "I have not sinned."

Religious sinners make God a liar. They deny that the God of the Bible is a God of truth. They acknowledge Jesus as a good teacher and a good man, but they deny that He is the eternal God who came to this world in flesh, lived a sinless life, died on the cross for the sins of mankind and rose from the dead on the third day. When people say they have not sinned, they deny the Jesus of the Bible.

If they do not admit their sins, then they are still in their sins. By denying that they are sinners they make God a liar, and His Word is not in them. They have turned from the light that would have led them to salvation and have gone into darkness, a darkness of their own choosing. Such people are lost. The light may shine around them, but they will not acknowledge the sin it exposes.

Cure by the Shed Blood

What is the remedy for this condition? The cure is suggested in I John 1:9. It lies in acknowledging the shed blood of Christ as it is presented in

25

Romans: "Being justified freely by his grace through the redemption that is in Christ Jesus: whom God hath set forth to be a propitiation through faith in his blood, to declare his righteousness for the remission of sins that are past, through the forbearance of God; to declare, I say, at this time his righteousness: that he might be just, and the justifier of him which believeth in Jesus" (3:24-26). Provision has been made in Christ for the forgiveness of sins. God is willing to pardon, to cancel the debt that is against sinners. When a sinner agrees with God that he needs Jesus Christ as Saviour, God will give him complete cleansing through Christ's shed blood.

Obedience the Test of Our Fellowship

"My little children, these things write I unto you, that ye sin not. And if any man sin, we have an advocate with the Father, Jesus Christ the righteous: and he is the propitiation for our sins: and not for our's only, but also for the sins of the whole world" (I John 2:1,2).

These two verses form a transition between the subject of Chapter 1 and the subject of Chapter 2. Chapter 1 showed how God's searchlight exposes sin; Chapter 2 shows how God's searchlight exposes the Christian's behavior. First John 2:1,2 covers both subjects—sin and the believer's behavior.

Grace Not a License to Sin

In the light of our exposition of Chapter 1, some might charge that it is easy to presume on the grace of God. Such is not the case. Paul said in Romans 5:20, "Moreover the law entered, that the offence might abound. But where sin abounded, grace did much more abound." He then had to defend the teaching of the Scripture against the false charge that abounding grace made it easy for persons to sin. He said in answer, "What shall we say then? Shall we continue in sin, that grace may abound? God forbid. How shall we that are dead to

27

sin, live any longer therein?" (6:1,2). So in I John, in order to offset anyone's presuming on the grace of God, John made this statement: "My little children, these things write I unto you, that ye sin not" (2:1). In treating this subject the apostle also showed how to maintain fellowship with God.

According to I John 1:9, the first step in restoring fellowship with God is confession of sins. First John 2:1 presents the fact that we are to forsake our sins. These two aspects of dealing with sin are summarized in Proverbs 28:13: "He that covereth his sins shall not prosper: but whoso confesseth and forsaketh them shall have mercy."

God's High Standard

First John 2:1 could be translated: "These things write I unto you that ye do not commit a single act of sin." John was not dealing with habitual sin but with single acts of sin. This is a high standard, and you may wonder if it is possible for a child of God to successfully live this way. Perhaps this can best be answered by realizing what Christ has actually done for us.

Christ, by becoming a partaker of flesh and blood and by being obedient to death, destroyed "him that had the power of death, that is, the devil" (Heb. 2:14). The same truth is taught in Revelation 12:11: "And they overcame him [Satan] by the blood of the Lamb." These verses clearly indicate that the power of Satan over us is broken and that though he may try to lead us into sin, we need not succumb to his allurements. Through Christ we have complete victory over the Evil One.

28

Furthermore, we learn from Galatians 5:16 that if we walk in the Spirit, we will not fulfill the lusts of the flesh. This also is victory—through the Holy Spirit. No wonder God's standard for us is that we should not sin.

In the light of our experience, however, this may well cause us to despair, for we realize that we do commit acts of sin. The next phrase in I John 2:1 says, "And if any man sin, we have an advocate with the Father, Jesus Christ the righteous." When we do commit an act of sin and Satan would accuse us before the Father, there is no way he can reach us because we stand before God in the righteousness of Christ, "even the righteousness of God which is by faith of Jesus Christ unto all and upon all them that believe: for there is no difference" (Rom. 3:22). So Jesus has become our righteousness, and He stands in the presence of God on our behalf.

Perhaps this can best be explained by the incident of Jesus' washing the disciples' feet. John's Gospel, Chapter 13, tells how the Saviour, after the supper ended, laid aside His garments, took a towel, poured water into a basin and began to wash the disciples' feet and to wipe them with the towel. Peter protested, but the Saviour said to him, "If I wash thee not, thou hast no part with me" (v. 8). Peter, realizing he had said the wrong thing but still not knowing what he was talking about, said, "Lord, not my feet only, but also my hands and my head" (v. 9).

The Lord answered him, "He that is washed needeth not save to wash his feet, but is clean every whit" (v. 10). The two words for "wash" in this verse do not refer to the same type of washing.

29

The first one has to do with a complete bath, whereas the second word refers to the cleansing of only a part of the body. The spiritual truth is that the person who has been washed in the blood of Jesus Christ from the guilt of sin, which is needed only once, needs a daily cleansing from the defilement of sin.

And so it is with us when we commit acts of sin and thus have our fellowship with God and our Saviour broken. We are restored to that fellowship when we confess our sin.

Christ Our Advocate

Let us look a little more closely at Christ as our Advocate. The word "Comforter," found in John 14:16, is the same word that is translated "advocate" in I John 2:1. In John 14:16 John was referring to the Holy Spirit, and in I John 2:1 he was referring to Jesus Christ. So we not only have an advocate who dwells within us to help us, to make intercession for us and to give us victory, but we also have a helper at the right hand of God—an advocate, or an attorney—to plead for us.

We have recognized that Christ is our Saviour from the condemnation of sin, but we see from this verse that He is our preserver and advocate when we commit acts of sin. And when He goes before the Father to plead for us, He does not plead our case but His own case. He died for our sins, and God, who is faithful and just to His Son and to the work He completed for us on Calvary, forgives us completely on the basis of His Son's work.

As a child of God the purpose of your heart is to live for Him; you want His life to be lived out in you. But you are weak and fall into sin. If such is the case, remember that He is your advocate. There is not only a faith that saves us from the condemnation of sin, but there is also a continuous faith whereby we are saved daily from the power of sin. If you feel that your faith has given out, then live by His faith. "I am crucified with Christ: nevertheless I live; yet not I, but Christ liveth in me: and the life which I now live in the flesh I live by the faith of the Son of God, who loved me, and gave himself for me" (Gal. 2:20).

The Basis of Christ's Advocacy

First John 2:2 explains how all this is possible: "And he is the propitiation for our sins: and not for our's only, but also for the sins of the whole world."

Additional light is given in Hebrews 9:22: "Without shedding of blood is no remission [of sin]." The blood that made the charge against us void was shed when Christ "appeared to put away sin by the sacrifice of himself" (v. 26). "By his own blood he entered in once into the holy place, having obtained eternal redemption for us" (v. 12). When His sacrifice is contrasted with those made under the Law, the record is "How much more shall the blood of Christ, who through the eternal Spirit offered himself without spot to God, purge your conscience from dead works to serve the living God?" (v. 14).

Sin stood between man and God. No fellowship was possible between us and Him until Christ removed that sin by the shedding of His blood. Now we can come wholeheartedly into God's presence. We can come boldly according to Hebrews 4:16 because Christ has made the way through His death for us. "Having therefore, brethren, boldness to enter into the holiest by the blood of Jesus, by a new and living way, which he hath consecrated for us, through the veil, that is to say, his flesh" (10:19,20). Through this way we come into the presence of God and enjoy His fellowship.

According to I John 2:2, Christ is not only the propitiation for the believer's sins, but also "for the sins of the whole world." Perhaps a better translation of this passage would be "But he is the propitiation for the whole world of sin." God's mercy is as wide as the sins of the world. If people do not experience its benefits, the fault does not lie with God but with them. He has made the provision. Christ died for all. No one is so great a sinner that Christ cannot save him.

Test by Obedience

Verse 3 of I John 2 introduces a different way of checking whether or not we are saved—the test by obedience. "And hereby we do know that we know him, if we keep his commandments. He that saith, I know him, and keepeth not his commandments, is a liar, and the truth is not in him. But whoso keepeth his word, in him verily is the love of God perfected: hereby know we that we are in him. He that saith he abideth in him ought himself also so to walk, even as he walked" (vv. 3-6). Notice the progression in these verses: knowing Him as Saviour, being in Him and abiding in Him.

Three Things We Know

When we keep His commandments, we know that we know Him. When we keep His Word, we know that we are in Him. When we walk as He walked, we know that we abide in Him.

We Know Him

We'll consider first the fact of knowing that we are saved. Expressed in I John 2:3 is the thought that we now know Him because at one time in the past we came to know Him through an event that has present results. That event, of course, was our spiritual rebirth, the event that marked the beginning of our Christian life. From that flow certain results in our present lives. One result is an inner living acquaintance with Him, proved by the fact that we keep His commandments.

There is a difference in thought and meaning between the word "keep" and the words "to do" His commandments. A person may do certain commands of God and yet not be saved. It is not possible, however, to keep the commandments of God and not be saved. The word "keep" refers to careful guarding and observing of the commandments. It involves the idea of an inner attitude toward the commandments whereby they are considered precious and, therefore, to be kept. This is vastly different from one who does something for fear of the consequences.

The driver who exceeds the speed limit and repeatedly glances in his rearview mirror to see if the patrolman is after him will obey the law if he must, but not because he wants to. The Christian keeps the commandments of Christ because he loves Christ and everything about Him. This may not always be true of the Christian, but the general quality of his life and the usual desire of his heart is to please the Lord.

There is also a contrast between the word "commandments" and the word "law." John never used the word "law" to refer to the Christian's principles of life. When he used the word "law," he referred to the Mosaic Law. When he wrote about commandments, however, he was speaking of the principles of the Christian life—the outworking of the Christ-life within us. Christ is the new life within us, and as we keep the commandments, we are giving outward expression and proof to the fact that we are born again.

John wrote in verse 5 of keeping "his word." There is a distinction between keeping the commandments and keeping the Word. Keeping the Word involves more than merely observing the stated precepts. It includes sensitivity to the mind of Christ expressed in the Word and to His work in our inner conscience through the Holy Spirit.

Suppose a number of children have been told to help their mother by washing the dishes. This they do, but they avoid doing anything extra, and as soon as they are finished, they run out to play without further regard for their mother's desires or wishes. But one child remains behind and asks his mother if there is something else he can do to help her. He has seen that his mother is tired. Even though she has given permission for them to leave, he wants to do more to help her because of his love and regard for her. This child is sensitive to his mother's needs—needs not expressed in her command to her children.

The person who says he knows God but does not keep His commandments and has no urge to please God is a liar, and the truth is not in him.

We Are in Him

Another proof of salvation and of Christian growth is revealed in I John 2:5: "Whoso keepeth his word, in him verily is the love of God perfected: hereby know we that we are in him." This goes a step beyond recognizing that we are closely united to Him. The love which has been shed abroad in our hearts (Rom. 5:5) has become active and has been perfected, or brought to maturity. We will study this subject of love more fully later.

We Abide in Him

Then there is this third important consideration for all Christians: "He that saith he abideth in him ought himself also so to walk, even as he walked" (I John 2:6). Here abiding is emphasized rather than works or doing. This progression in the Christian life is illustrated in Israel's history. She was first delivered from guilt and condemnation through the blood of the Passover lamb in Egypt. Then she experienced the power of God as she was trained and cared for in the desert. Finally, the perfecting of God's work in her was seen when she was brought into the land and dwelt there. This word "abide" means to remain. This does not mean just to have a place but to enjoy fellowship,

35

communion, harmony and friendship with all who are in that place.

Abiding in Him is not imitating Him but is letting His life flow in and through us. As a result we will walk as He walked. He walked with unwavering faith. Is that characteristic of our faith? If our faith is wavering, then we are not abiding. Unwavering faith is the result of living in communion with Him.

Jesus walked in total submission to the Father. He said it was His food to do the Father's will (see John 4:34). Likewise, when we do the will of God, we are sure to be abiding in Christ. Self can have no part in such a life.

Our Saviour's walk was marked by grace and humility. He lived for the benefit of others. When we abide in Him, we will have steadfast perseverance. Even when suffering, we will learn to be patient. All of this will prove that we are abiding in Him. Remember, however, that none of this is possible unless it is done in the power of the Holy Spirit who dwells within us.

The New Commandment

"Brethren, I write no new commandment unto you, but an old commandment which ye had from the beginning. The old commandment is the word which ye have heard from the beginning. Again, a new commandment I write unto you, which thing is true in him and in you: because the darkness is past, and the true light now shineth" (I John 2:7,8).

The statements concerning the old and the new commandment sound paradoxical. They can be readily reconciled, however. The Apostle John wrote here, as the following verses show, about our love for one another. In a sense this is not a new commandment; it is an old one that goes back to the time when God made man in His own image. Since man was made in the image of God, love was part of the expression of his life. It is old also in the sense that the Old Testament Law was summarized in the commands to love God and love our neighbor.

From all of this one might conclude that there is nothing new about this commandment at all, and yet there is an aspect that is new. We are given the clue to this in the expression, "The darkness is past, and the true light now shineth" (v. 8). Here again the present tense was used, and the translation could read: "The darkness is passing, and the true light is now shining." Under the Old Testament Law, people were commanded to love, but the Law did not provide them with the ability to obey. Only as the Holy Spirit could get control of individual hearts was this possible. But the Lord Jesus came into this world as the light to dispel the darkness. He showed sin to be sin in a way that people had not realized before, but He also came to give the life that would enable them to fulfill completely His purposes in them.

This is clearly seen in the individual experience of each believer who begins the Christian life with only a slight grasp of the real knowledge of both sin and righteousness, but as he grows in the Christian life the darkness begins to be dispelled and the true light shines brighter and brighter.

All that the Law could show was that people were sinful and dwelling in darkness, but Christ

37

came to produce righteousness, light and life. That is the new thing spoken of in I John 2:7,8.

Hating a Brother

The apostle used an illustration to help clarify this subject. He said, "He that saith he is in the light, and hateth his brother, is in darkness even until now. He that loveth his brother abideth in the light, and there is none occasion of stumbling in him" (I John 2:9,10). This word "hate" is a very strong word meaning malicious and unjustifiable feelings against another person. This hatred can be present in the heart, even though it is not expressed in actions: "Whosoever hateth his brother is a murderer: and ye know that no murderer hath eternal life abiding in him" (3:15). We usually think of murder as an act, but God describes it as an inward feeling, or attitude, against another person. Such an attitude may lead to the act of murder if left unchecked.

Loving a Brother

The word for "love" in I John 2:10 is the strongest word used in the Bible to describe love. It involves more than an impulsive feeling or even the love of a wife for her husband or a mother for her children. It is the kind of love that describes God Himself: "God is love" (4:8). God, as to His nature, is love.

This kind of love thinks no evil and does no evil to others (see I Cor. 13:5). Therefore, "love is the fulfilling of the law" (Rom. 13:10). It is the kind of love spoken of in John 3:16: "God so

38

loved the world, that he gave his only begotten
Son." It is a supernaturally produced love and is
shed abroad in our hearts by the Holy Spirit (see
Rom. 5:5).

Do we love the Lord and love others?

Worldliness

The new and yet old commandment concerning love is seen negatively in this section of our
study. The admonition is "Love not the world,
neither the things that are in the world. If any man
love the world, the love of the Father is not in him.
For all that is in the world, the lust of the flesh,
and the lust of the eyes, and the pride of life, is not
of the Father, but is of the world. And the world
passeth away, and the lust thereof: but he that
doeth the will of God abideth for ever" (I John
2:15-17).

Worldliness Defined

In seeking to define "worldliness" we must
first define the word "world." John was not speaking of this earth but of the world system on the
earth. This is an ordered system which Satan rules
with his demons and other powers. The members
of the unsaved human race are his subjects.

When Satan tempted the Lord Jesus and promised to give Him the world if He would fall down
and worship him, he was talking about the organ-
ized system of which he, Satan, is the ruler. Consequently, when we talk about worldliness, we are
not speaking of something material but of a way of
life that is opposed to God's way. In Ephesians 2

39

Paul described the former life of the Christian as the time when he "walked according to the course of this world, according to the prince of the power of the air, the spirit that now worketh in the children of disobedience" (v. 2). There are worldly things, but worldliness itself involves more than things and goes far beyond anything that we ordinarily consider to be worldly.

To some people worldliness involves only things. Of course, they cannot agree on what things are worldly since they miss the point that worldliness is primarily an attitude of heart. Wearing certain things and going to certain places is worldly to some, while to others it is not. We must see something more basic before we become too involved in trying to classify things as being worldly.

Someone has said, "Worldliness is present when things make us lose our joy. When the coming or going of things causes our true joy to cease, we have become worldly."

Worldliness Expressed

Worldliness can be expressed by nations or by individuals as greed. Such greed at times leads to violent action both on the part of nations and of individuals in order to gain their ends. This all comes from Satan and not from God.

It is easy to be tripped by worldliness. Even looking for praise for something good that we have done could indicate worldliness. There is a normal place for appreciation for another's services in our lives, but for ourselves we must recognize that whatever good we do comes through God and not from our own strength.

Ambition in itself is not necessarily wrong, but it can be worldly, depending on our motives. If our ambition is something for self, then that is worldliness. Pleasure and recreation have a place, but be sure they do not take you away from God.

Ask yourself these questions: What is the purpose of my life? What am I going after? What are my pleasures? What are my practices? What kind of places do I frequent? Could I invite God to look with approval on all that I do and seek for?

Worldliness in its final analysis is an attitude of heart toward things and persons. It is the old-nature attitude and can affect every phase of our lives.

Our Sole Aim in Life

As children of God we should have but one purpose in life—to be witnesses for Jesus Christ. Everything else has to work in harmony with that.

But someone will say, "I am a farmer" or "I am a businessman" or "I'm a factory worker." You can still be a witness for the Lord Jesus. God has placed you in that particular spot for that purpose. Not everybody can be a preacher, but every Christian can be a witness. So it all comes down to what our motives are and what we are doing.

It has helped me to remember that wherever I go God goes with me. As a young man I followed certain practices from which I was delivered when I realized that I was indwelt by Christ.

Many things are outwardly religious but can be worldly, depending on our motive in practicing them.

In John 7:7 the Saviour, speaking to certain

persons who did not believe in Him, said, "The world cannot hate you; but me it hateth, because I testify of it, that the works thereof are evil." Then, speaking to His disciples, the Saviour said, "If ye were of the world, the world would love his own: but because ye are not of the world, but I have chosen you out of the world, therefore the world hateth you" (15:19). The believer is chosen out from the world. He is not to be part of the world system, and for this reason, the world is bound to hate him.

Love Not the World

We are told in I John not to love the world (2:15). We have considered the word "love" already, but we have not exhausted its meaning. God loved us so much that He gave His Son for us. In this verse He is telling us not to love the world or its attractions with this kind of love. In effect, He is saying, "Do not love these things or the world system that sponsors them."

Money is a necessary commodity for living. Nothing is wrong with money in itself, but the love of money is dangerous (see I Tim. 6:10). If we set our hearts on acquiring money for money's sake, then we are worldly and loving the things of the world instead of God. We cannot love the world and have love for God in our hearts too.

The more I love the things of the world, the less of God's love there can possibly be in me. That is why we are told: "Be not conformed to this world: but be ye transformed by the renewing of your mind" (Rom. 12:2). James said, "Know ye not that the friendship of the world is enmity with God? Whosoever therefore will be a friend of the world is the enemy of God" (James 4:4).

One of the purposes in Christ's death was "that he might deliver us from this present evil world" (Gal. 1:4). And in Colossians Paul said, "Who hath delivered us from the power of darkness" (1:13).

Three Dangerous Things in the World

John said there are three things in the world that we must watch out for—the lust of the flesh, the lust of the eyes and the pride of life. The word "lust" does not necessarily mean something evil. The context helps to determine whether it is used in a good sense or a bad one. The word itself means a passionate desire or a craving after something. In this passage it is used in a bad sense, and we are warned first of all to not have a passionate craving for, or a reaching after, things of the flesh, which is the old nature.

The eyes must be carefully guarded. We are warned concerning the lust of the eyes, or the strong, passionate desires which arise because of what the eyes see. A great deal of our present-day advertising is built on eye appeal and is designed to stimulate our baser passions.

The lust of the eyes may take another form. We may see something that somebody has and want it. That desire may consume our waking thoughts and destroy our fellowship with God.

The pride of life incorporates the idea of one who claims credit and glory for something that is not really his. We can see it very clearly in the person who constantly brags about his own resources and possessions.

But this kind of pride may take another turn. Because we do not do certain things in our particular church group or because we do not wear certain things or go to certain places, we may look down on others who do and think in pride that we are living closer to God. That is part of the pride of life, and it is worldliness. If Satan can keep us from doing certain things, he will also get us to be proud of the fact that we are not doing them. God warns, "The world passeth away, and the lust thereof: but he that doeth the will of God abideth for ever" (I John 2:17).

The Test by Belief

First John 2:18-28 covers a subject that is very vital in our day. The passage begins: "Little children, it is the last time: and as ye have heard that antichrist shall come, even now are there many antichrists; whereby we know that it is the last time. They went out from us, but they were not of us; for if they had been of us, they would no doubt have continued with us: but they went out, that they might be made manifest that they were not all of us . . . . Who is a liar but he that denieth that Jesus is the Christ? He is antichrist, that denieth the Father and the Son" (vv. 18,19,22).

The question of who is a true believer and who is a pretender is tested from the standpoint of doctrine. And the doctrine at issue is the Person of Christ Himself. There is a play on the two words "Jesus" and "Christ," and some may wonder why.

The name "Christ" indicated that Jesus is the anointed, eternal Son of God. His eternal existence and His power are implied in this name. In other words, Christ is the eternal God who came in the flesh. The name "Jesus," meaning "Saviour," emphasized His humanity.

Many people will acknowledge a historical Jesus. They admit that He lived in this world, and they give great acclaim to His teaching. They speak much about His teaching on love, but they deny that He was and is the eternal God. Such persons are not born-again Christians. They may participate in many religious activities, but the Bible describes them as "antichrists." That is not a pleasant name, but that is the one God uses to describe those who deny that Jesus is the Christ.

Antichrists Not Born Again

We are able to detect who these antichrists are: "They went out from us, but they were not of us" (I John 2:19). This does not mean that they left a particular denomination or church. They left the fundamental doctrine of Jesus Christ. The Word says they were never born again. Verse 19 makes that abundantly clear. The words "no doubt" are in italics in some translations, indicating that they were added by the translators. Consequently, the verse actually says, "They went out from us, but they were not of us; for if they had been of us, they would have continued with us."

This is fundamental to our whole understanding of the Christian life. If these people had been

45

true believers in Christ, they would have received eternal life, which is Christ Himself dwelling within the believer. The Lord Jesus said in John 10:27, "My sheep hear my voice, and I know them, and they follow me." He was speaking of His own children, those who are truly born again. He then declared, "I give unto them eternal life" (v. 28). That is a new kind of life, the kind of life that only God can produce in a person.

Being recipients of eternal life, "they shall never perish, neither shall any man pluck them out of my hand," the Saviour said. "My Father, which gave them me, is greater than all; and no man is able to pluck them out of my Father's hand. I and my Father are one" (vv. 28-30). The person who has eternal life cannot be taken away from God.

A true child of God will not accept any doctrine that denies that Jesus was and is the eternal God. A person who says that Jesus is not God is not a child of God and cannot go to heaven.

Of God's children we read: "Who are kept by the power of God through faith unto salvation ready to be revealed in the last time" (I Pet. 1:5).

In I John 2, we are told that we have received an anointing, an unction, from the Holy One and that we know all things (see v. 20). At salvation the Holy Spirit came to live in us, and He will never allow us to be taken away and seduced with doctrines that teach that Jesus is not the true, living, eternal Son of God.

False Teaching of Antichrists

Those who are termed "antichrists" may speak much of the fatherhood of God and the brotherhood of man, but they do not present their ideas from the biblical standpoint, for they are not members of God's family.

The false teachers described in this passage do not teach the total depravity of man. They will say that there is something good and commendable in man. They will speak of a divine spark or something similar, but there is no spiritual spark in the heart of man. There is no spiritual life in anyone until he or she trusts Christ as personal Saviour.

These false teachers may tell us to have faith in ourselves, but that is not what God tells us to do. God says that we should place no faith in man but should put our faith in Jesus Christ (see Jer. 17:5).

False teachers will also deny the efficacy of the shed blood of Christ, but the Scriptures teach that without the shedding of blood there is no remission of sin (Heb. 9:22).

These false teachers will deny the necessity of the new birth and claim that all people have to do is follow Jesus as an example. But John 3:3 says, "Except a man be born again, he cannot see the kingdom of God." This applies to all people, not just to a few.

In I John 2:28 we are given a warning that is needed at all times. One day the Saviour will come, and surely we do not want to be ashamed before Him at His coming. Surely we would not be satisfied to be saved "so as by fire" (I Cor. 3:15). Instead, we will seek for an abundant entrance into His kingdom. For this to be a reality, we must use all the resources He has placed at our disposal so that we might grow and prosper in things that pertain to life and godliness (II Pet. 1:3).

Salvation Tested by Love

Chapter 3 of I John introduces love as the test of an individual's salvation. This test grows out of the fact that the Father has bestowed love on His children, and they in turn exhibit that love to others (see Rom. 5:5).

Standing of Two Spiritual Families

The first ten verses of I John 3 relate to the standing of the children of God in contrast to the standing of the children of the Devil. There are basically two spiritual families in the world, although some would tell us that we are all the children of God. They glibly quote Galatians 3:26 but use only half of the verse: "Ye are all the children of God." They conveniently forget that the second half, "by faith in Christ Jesus," qualifies the first. Our Saviour once said to such people, "Ye are of your father the devil" (John 8:44). And John wrote: "In this the children of God are manifest, and the children of the devil" (I John 3:10).

Verse 1 of this section brings before us the subject of the believer's standing: "Behold, what manner of love the Father hath bestowed upon us, that we should be called the sons of God: therefore the world knoweth us not, because it knew him not." Our standing is emphasized in the expression "called the sons [children] of God."

Our standing with God refers to our relationship to Him, not to our fellowship. Our standing is our position in heaven before God in Christ; whereas our state is our behavior, or conduct, here on the earth.

The standing of a child in a family involves the fact that the child belongs to the family. The child's state relates to his conduct, good or bad. The behavior of the child brings either honor or dishonor to the family name. But whether or not he contributes honor, he is still a child in the family.

Some may object and say, "But the children can be disinherited." This is true, but disinheritance does not change the standing of that child in the family. Only his fellowship, his rewards and his inheritance can be changed. The fact that he was born into the family cannot be changed.

Standing and State Illustrated

We must understand this in the spiritual realm. Through Christ we were reconciled to God and were given a standing in righteousness before Him. We became His children through faith in Christ, through a spiritual birth (see John 3:3-6).

First John 3:2 says that since we are the children of God, we shall one day be made like the Saviour. This is our "hope," and we are informed that this hope will affect our state: "Every man that hath this hope in him purifieth himself, even as he is pure" (v. 3). The conclusion is inescapable,

50

then, that because of a believer's standing, his state, or behavior, will be purified. If he does not have a standing with God in Christ, then no such change in his life and conduct will be evident.

We can see this principle very clearly in the life of Abraham. God made a covenant with him, which is recorded in Genesis 12 and 15. But it was a one-sided covenant based on God's keeping it and Abraham's receiving it. That is similar to our salvation, for it is provided by God, and He is responsible for keeping us. Our responsibility is to receive it by faith.

The promise to Abraham was sevenfold and related in some of its aspects to the land of Palestine. Even though Abraham later left Palestine and went to Egypt, God did not forget His promise to him. And even though years later Israel was scattered among the nations because of misconduct and unbelief, God never rescinded His promise concerning the land or the people. The nations have never been able to destroy Israel, and today the Israelites are returning to the land promised to Abraham. God never changes, and "the gifts and calling of God are without repentance [change of mind]" (Rom. 11:29).

So it is with our salvation. The promise concerning our salvation, which we received by faith, is not revoked because we sometimes fall into sin. To maintain our union with the Father we have an advocate, Jesus Christ the righteous (see I John 2:1).

The works that we do, the kind of lives we live and our behavior after we are saved will demonstrate the fact that we are saved. Our works do not make us children of God, but they show that we are His children. Again this is illustrated by Abraham's life: "Was not Abraham our father justified by works, when he had offered Isaac his son upon the altar?" (James 2:21). This event happened long after Abraham was justified by faith. This act was a demonstration of Abraham's obedience to God and was proof of the new life within him.

This event in Abraham's life is also spoken of in Hebrews 11: "By faith Abraham, when he was tried, offered up Isaac: and he that had received the promises offered up his only begotten son. Of whom it was said, That in Isaac shall thy seed be called: accounting that God was able to raise him up, even from the dead; from whence also he received him in a figure" (vv. 17-19). So Abraham demonstrated his new life in this act of obedience.

It is well to remember, however, that both Abraham and his posterity, the Children of Israel, were always disciplined by God for misconduct. So it is with us. "Whom the Lord loveth he chasteneth, and scourgeth every son whom he receiveth" (12:6).

Standing and State of Unbelievers

In contrast, notice the standing and state of the children of the Devil. It is partially indicated by the expression, "the world knoweth us not, because it knew him not" (I John 3:1). The world does not know God because it has a different father. "If God were your Father, ye would love me: for I proceeded forth and came from God" (John 8:42). To that same group the Saviour said,

"Ye are of your father the devil" (v. 44). Then in verse 47 He said, "He that is of God heareth God's words: ye therefore hear them not, because ye are not of God." These people failed to recognize that Jesus was the Son of God. The actions demonstrating their state were in conformity to their standing, for their spiritual ignorance was due to their spiritual heredity. The children of the world cannot know our Lord. Only as they respond to the revealed Word of God and to the Spirit of God and receive Jesus Christ as Saviour can their standing and their state be changed.

Abiding

The person who has the hope of Christ's return in his heart purifies himself. The Scriptures do not say that he ought to or that he should, but it says that he does (see I John 3:2,3).

For this to be fulfilled in us we must abide in fellowship with the Lord. The word "abiding" does not refer to keeping salvation, for our salvation is kept by the power of God. That is what God has done for us. Then through our abiding, God can do certain things in us. When we abide in Him, we take all things that concern our lives to Him as a child would go to a parent. A child goes to his parents with all his cares, hurts, complaints and enjoyments. So it is with us—we take our problems, our trials and our needs to Him. We also share our joys with Him.

The child who does not abide is disciplined by God. In the previous chapter are these significant words: "And now, little children, abide in him; that, when he shall appear, we may have confidence, and not be ashamed before him at his coming" (2:28). If we abide in Him, there will be no need for shame when we see Him.

Through the new birth we have received a new nature from God, but as long as we are in this body we will also have the old nature with us. This means that there is a constant conflict between the two: "The flesh lusteth against the Spirit, and the Spirit against the flesh: and these are contrary the one to the other" (Gal. 5:17). We are on the victory side, however, and need not be defeated in this conflict.

When the Lord comes, we shall be rid of the old nature, and "we shall be like him; for we shall see him as he is" (I John 3:2).

We long for that day as did the Apostle Paul: "And not only they, but ourselves also, which have the firstfruits of the Spirit, even we ourselves groan within ourselves, waiting for the adoption, to wit, the redemption of our body" (Rom. 8:23).

The Holy Spirit has been given to us, and He is the earnest of our inheritance until complete redemption is given us at the coming of our Saviour (see Eph. 1:12-14). Our bodies will be redeemed from this sin-cursed earth, and we will no longer be harassed by the tests of sin and the opposition of Satan. (Read also Phil. 3:21; John 14:1-6; I Thess. 4:13-18; I Cor. 15:51-57.)

A true scriptural grasp of this hope of the Lord's return will not create in us a desire to merely escape this world and its present troubles, but rather it will have a purifying effect on us, for we will want to be ready to meet the Saviour when He appears.

A Misunderstood Portion

Many false doctrines have been built on I John 3:4-10. Part of this may be due to the fact that some translations are not quite clear. Some have used these verses to teach that a person reaches a certain place in his Christian life after which he no longer commits any sin. These verses do not give any license to sin, but they contrast the state, or behavior, of the children of God with the state, or behavior, of the children of the world. The behavior of a child of God is the result of his right standing with God and not the means to that right standing.

Another false doctrine that some have formulated is that if we live right, God will accept us. That is impossible. We are accepted by God only on the merits of the Lord Jesus and His finished work on Calvary. As a result of accepting Christ's provision of salvation by faith, God produces in us a life that honors Him.

These verses disclose the relation of the Christian to sin. They also show that the manifestation of the new life in Christ becomes a means of testing whether or not we have the right standing with God.

State of the Saved Contrasted With State of the Lost

The present tense is used extensively in I John 3:4-10, and in the Greek that tense means more than something done in present time. It conveys the idea of continual, habitual action. For instance, "whosoever committeth sin" (v. 4) should be translated "whosoever continues to live in sin" or "whosoever habitually sins." In verse 6 the phrase "whosoever abideth in him sinneth not" should be "whosoever continually abides in him will not be habitually sinning." This simply means that because we are born again and are the children of God, we are prevented from habitually living in sin. It is impossible for a person who is born again to continually exhibit only sin and never righteousness in his life.

In contrast to this is the expression in I John 2:1: "These things write I unto you, that ye sin not." Here the tense is not the present but the aorist. This verse is best translated: "These things write I unto you, that you do not commit an act of sin." Here acts of sin are considered, not sin as a habit and life principle.

Why the Believer Does Not Practice Sin

To live under the dominion of sin without any evidence of righteousness demonstrates that the person has not been born again. The reasons for this are clearly pointed out in some of these verses. First John 3:4, for example, says that sin is contrary to the law of God. Verse 5 says that sin is contrary to the mission, or the work, of the Lord Jesus Christ. Christ not only came to take away the guilt of sin, but He broke sin's power so that the believer need not live under its dominion. When we do commit an act of sin and then confess it, God is faithful and just to forgive our sins, and our advocate with the Father maintains our standing of righteousness before Him.

The believer cannot habitually live in sin because such a life is not in accord with his union with Christ. We are told, "Whosoever [habitually] sinneth hath not seen him, neither known him" (v. 6).

The new life in Christ produces righteousness. Verse 7 says, "He that [habitually] doeth righteousness is righteous, even as he [Jesus] is righteous."

We must remember that there are degrees of growth in the Christian life. God works in us "both to will and to do of his good pleasure" (Phil. 2:13), which is a declaration that God gives us the desire to live righteously. If a person does not have this desire, even though he claims to know God, there is good reason for him to question whether or not he is really a child of God. Through abiding in Him maturity is produced in the Christian's life. This is not a goal that may be reached overnight, but God will produce it in us as we continually yield ourselves to Him.

A continual practice of sin in the life shows that the person is a child of the Devil rather than a child of God. "The devil sinneth from the beginning" (I John 3:8), and his children continue to live in sin, for that is in keeping with the character of their heredity.

Christ Delivers From the Power of Sin

First John 3:5 says, "And ye know that he was manifested to take away our sins; and in him is no sin." We know that Christ came to save us from the guilt and condemnation of our sin. That is why we

57

are told in Romans 8:1: "There is therefore now no condemnation to them which are in Christ Jesus."

Christ also broke the power of sin and delivered us from its slavery. "Sin shall not have dominion over you: for ye are not under the law, but under grace" (6:14). Sin can no longer be our master; we are no longer its slaves. The reason for this is given in the first part of Romans 6: "What shall we say then? Shall we continue in [habitual] sin, that grace may abound? God forbid. How shall we that are dead to sin, live any longer therein?" (vv. 1,2). Verses 6 and 7 also help to clarify this principle: "Knowing this, that our old self was crucified with Him, that our body of sin might be done away with, that we should no longer be slaves to sin; for he who has died is freed from sin" (NASB).

When a loved one dies, that one can show no response to us, even if we stand around the coffin weeping and trying to speak to him. We are alive, but the loved one is dead to us. So it is in the spiritual realm. Through our union with Christ we have died to sin. It has no further claim on us. We, being dead to it, need no longer respond to it.

When our Saviour died, He broke the power of sin and released the souls that were under bondage to the Evil One (see Heb. 2:14,15). Daily we must claim that great fact, recognizing that in ourselves we do not have the power to overcome sin. We can find the power only in Christ. As we abide in Him from moment to moment and day to day, we find victory over sin and live righteously.

What we have said so far should help us understand I John 3:9: "Whosoever is born of God doth not [continually] commit sin; for his seed remaineth in him: and he cannot sin, because he is born of God." That seed is the principle of divine life, that divine nature which God gives us when we are born again. This causes us to hate sin and to love righteousness. The presence of this seed makes it impossible for us who are born again to habitually live in sin or to habitually practice sin.

This divine principle, or seed, is not in the unsaved. Some people talk about the divine spark in the human heart, but there is no such thing. The Christian receives this seed at the new birth, and it remains in him. This is what God says, and we must take God at His word.

What Is Backsliding?

Some may wonder just what backsliding is. Backsliding is a lack of growth. For example, we may plant a seed in the ground, but because of lack of moisture it may be hindered from growing. A natural seed can die, and a natural plant can die. Spiritual life may be hindered in growth, but it cannot be killed. First John 2:19 says, "They went out from us, but they were not of us." They did not have the divine seed within them.

Verse 10 of I John 3 is a climax to this section. It shows that the tests we have been considering provide the proof as to who are the children of God and who are the children of the Devil. The one who does not practice righteousness is not of God, and the one who practices righteousness is of God.

Reasons From Romans

Set forth in Romans 8 are a number of reasons why a Christian does not continually practice sin but does practice righteousness. Notice in verse 1 that a born-again child of God is free from the condemnation of sin. Through Christ believers are made free.

Verse 2 tells us that the law of the Spirit of life in Christ Jesus has made us free from the law of sin and death. The Christian is freed from sin's enslavement. In Israel's experience this was illustrated at the Red Sea when they were separated not only from the people of Egypt, but God also broke the power of Egypt over them by removing its leaders and army.

A third statement is found in verse 3: "For what the law could not do, in that it was weak through the flesh, God sending his own Son in the likeness of sinful flesh, and for sin, condemned sin in the flesh." When Christ took on Himself the sins of mankind, God condemned, dethroned and broke the power of that sinful nature. That does not mean that sin was eradicated, but its power was broken through the finished work of Christ on Calvary.

A dictator may be deposed from his place of authority and flee into exile. Though he no longer has reigning power in the country from which he fled, he, in one way or another, may keep his former subjects in a state of agitation and turmoil. God has deposed the old nature and its power. He has broken its authority. Though we listen to it at times and, of course, get into trouble because of it, the old nature really has no right to control us.

The new nature, which is Christ in us, produces a godly life. For this reason it is possible for the Christian to walk according to the will of God. The righteousness that the Law required is fulfilled in the believer who walks after the Spirit and not after the flesh (v. 4). When a person walks after the Spirit, the Spirit can produce the godly life in him (see Gal. 5:16).

Still another statement is made in Romans 8:5: "For they that are after the flesh do mind the things of the flesh; but they that are after the Spirit the things of the Spirit." The word "mind" is an important word in this verse. It means that those who follow the old nature are earthly minded while those who follow the Spirit are spiritually minded.

To be earthly minded results in death, but to be spiritually minded results in life and peace (v. 6). So if our minds are still continually following and reaching after the things of the world, we are still living under the dominion of sin. The person who is spiritually minded may get out of fellowship with God at times, but because of the work of the Lord, he will be brought back into fellowship again.

In order to bring encouragement the Apostle Paul wrote: "But ye are not in the flesh, but in the Spirit, if so be that the Spirit of God dwell in you. Now if any man have not the Spirit of Christ, he is none of his. And if Christ be in you, the body is dead because of sin; but the Spirit is life because of righteousness" (vv. 9,10). You cannot be a Christian unless you have the Holy Spirit within, and when anyone accepts the Lord Jesus Christ as Saviour, the Holy Spirit indwells that person.

In verse 11 we read these words: "But if the Spirit of him that raised up Jesus from the dead dwell in you, he that raised up Christ from the dead shall also quicken your mortal bodies by his Spirit that dwelleth in you." Paul was not referring to the final resurrection of the body. That he discussed later in this chapter. In verse 11 he referred to bringing life (energy) into our bodies now so that we can do the will of God and not have to obey the flesh, or the old nature.

If we live after the flesh, we shall die (v. 13). This is not the kind of death that condemns us, for there is no condemnation for those in Christ Jesus. It is a death involving fellowship with God. When the flesh controls us, we are dead to God just as darkness is dead to light. The remedy is given in verse 13: "If ye through the Spirit do mortify the deeds of the body, ye shall live."

Imputed and Practical Righteousness

We have seen from various passages in I John that the believer practices righteousness, or habitually does righteous things. This does not mean that his righteous acts are merely occasional. Because of the new life within, it is his nature to do what pleases God.

The unbeliever, on the other hand, is under the domination of his fallen nature and does not practice righteousness but sin. He cannot practice righteousness until he is born of God.

There is in Scripture a vast difference between what is sometimes called imputed righteousness and practical, or imparted, righteousness. Imputed righteousness is righteousness that has been put to our account through faith in Christ's finished work. We are not saved by doing righteous deeds, but the practicing of righteousness comes as a result of having been saved.

The need for imputed righteousness is very clearly brought out by Paul's discussion of Israel in Romans 10. He said he was greatly concerned about them. He wanted them to be saved (v. 1). They were a religious people, and from the standpoint of the world, they did many good things. Paul listed some of those things, such as a zeal for God (v. 2). But this very zeal for God was standing in the way of their being saved through the imputed righteousness that God wanted to give them. They were ignorant of God's righteousness and tried to establish their own righteousness. They refused to submit themselves to the righteousness of God (v. 3). "Christ is the end of the law for righteousness to every one that believeth" (v. 4).

The subject of John's first epistle, however, is not imputed righteousness but practical righteousness, or right living. When I was born again, I became a member of the Body of Christ. My hand is a member of my body; therefore, it is obedient to me. It is as strong as I can possibly make it, and if I want to lift something, it will do it for me. Why? Because it obeys the orders that my mind sends to it.

As a member of the Body of Jesus Christ, His life flows through me; and when He desires something, I do it. Of course, there are times when disobedience occurs. We fail the Lord. But when we are convicted of that fact, then we confess our sin, are restored to fellowship and go on in obedience. Responding to the will of the Lord becomes the habit of the Christian life because of the new life in Christ.

A vital contrast, then, between a child of the Devil and a child of God is that the child of God has both imputed righteousness and practical righteousness. The child of the Devil, on the other hand, has no righteousness but seeks to make himself right with God on the basis of his works, which, of course, is an impossible goal.

Presence or Absence of Love

Another contrast between believers and unbelievers involves love. Verse 10 of I John 3 says, "Whosoever doeth not righteousness is not of God, neither he that loveth not his brother." The lack of love on the part of the unbeliever and the presence of love on the part of the believer makes the contrast. Verse 11 says, "For this is the message that ye heard from the beginning, that we should love one another." This word for "love" does not refer to a sentimental love but is a strong word that describes God Himself. It is the kind of love that recognizes a need and responds to that need.

An illustration of this contrast is seen in the case of Cain, who was of the Wicked One and killed his brother (v. 12). He killed Abel because his own works were evil and his brother's were righteous. Cain did not have love in his heart because he was not a child of God. He had hatred, and for that reason he murdered Abel.

"We know that we have passed from death unto life, because we love the brethren. He that loveth not his brother abideth in death. Whosoever hateth his brother is a murderer: and ye know that no murderer hath eternal life abiding in him" (vv. 14,15). A mark of the Christian, then, is that he loves other believers (all born-again ones). This is a much needed reminder for us in this day.

Because the Scriptures say that no murderer has eternal life abiding in him, we need not conclude that a murderer cannot be saved. He can be if he will come to Christ and receive Him as Saviour.

Love for the Brethren

First John 3:16 shows that true love is climaxed by our being willing to lay down our lives for fellow believers. This is the very opposite of being willing to slander and spread evil reports concerning God's children. This kind of love is very practical, for John said, "But whoso hath this world's good, and seeth his brother have need, and shutteth up his bowels of compassion from him, how dwelleth the love of God in him?" (v. 17). God expects us to share the temporal and spiritual provisions that He makes for us. How can anyone, looking on this lost world, say that he loves the Lord and yet not seek to make known to the unsaved the unsearchable riches of Christ?

God and the Christian's Conscience

This Book of I John is one of intimate fellowship, and it is no wonder that the expression "we know" often occurs. In verse 19 John said, "Hereby we know that we are of the truth, and shall assure our hearts before him." We not only can know truth with our minds, but we can also have assurance of it in our hearts. However, regardless of our feelings or prejudices about any truth, we must believe God for what He says.

Verse 20 adds: "For if our heart condemn us, God is greater than our heart, and knoweth all things." The subject here is assurance to the heart, or the conscience. The conscience is not always a safe guide. A matter may not be right, even though our conscience has failed to condemn us for it, but God is greater than our conscience. He may say very directly through the Word that we are not living in a manner pleasing to Him.

On the other hand, a person's conscience may not be properly trained, and it may condemn him for doing things that are not in themselves wrong. Or he may have a conscience that responds to one thing but is blind to another.

Paul persecuted the church and thought he was doing God a service. But when he met the Lord Jesus face to face, he realized how wrong he had been. God is greater than all our consciences. He knows all things. We must train our consciences in accordance with the Word.

Prayer

The last three verses in I John 3 are very important: "And whatsoever we ask, we receive of him, because we keep his commandments, and do those things that are pleasing in his sight. And this is his commandment, That we should believe on the name of his Son Jesus Christ, and love one another, as he gave us commandment. And he that keepeth his commandments dwelleth in him, and he in him. And hereby we know that he abideth in us, by the Spirit which he hath given us" (vv. 22-24).

Do the Scriptures tell us that God will answer our prayers only if we live sinlessly perfect lives? If we take this portion by itself and do not compare it with other passages on the subject of prayer, we might conclude that no one could have his prayers answered.

Some other scriptures will help us: "If ye abide in me, and my words abide in you, ye shall ask what ye will, and it shall be done unto you" (John 15:7). "Ye have not chosen me, but I have chosen you, and ordained you, that ye should go and bring forth fruit, and that your fruit should remain: that whatsoever ye shall ask of the Father in my name, he may give it you" (v. 16). "And whatsoever ye shall ask in my name, that will I do, that the Father may be glorified in the Son. If ye shall ask any thing in my name, I will do it" (14:13,14).

None of these scriptures teach that we merit the answers to our prayers by doing certain things, such as keeping the Ten Commandments. What God asks is that we put our trust in His name. First John deals with what we are in Christ Jesus, and it is the name of our Saviour that is powerful.

What does it mean to keep His commandments? Some say it is the law of Christ, but what is the law of Christ? It is "Christ in you, the hope of glory" (Col. 1:27).

His commandment is that we believe on the name of His Son, Jesus Christ. What is involved in that? First, we have forgiveness of our sins. Second, He is our life; therefore, it would be utterly impossible for us to come to God apart from Jesus Christ. He is our life—He is risen and is seated at the right hand of God on our behalf today.

Through His power and through His name we receive answers to prayer.

But some ask, "Does He not have other commandments? Did He not say in John 15:7, 'If ye abide in me'?" What is it, then, to abide in Him? It is simply to believe in His name and to trust Him for everything. If we fail on some point, we must turn to Him, believing that He forgives our failures. That is why He is at the right hand of God. That is why He said that if we confess our sins, we are then restored to fellowship. (Read I John 1:9; Heb. 7:25; I John 1:6,7.)

Another factor involved here is that His words must abide in us. As we come to know the Word and obey the Spirit through the Word, God can answer prayer. We must believe, of course, that Christ is our Lord, submit to Him and trust Him in everything. Then loving others will be a natural result of our life of trust in Him.

Chapter 4

Warning Against False Teachers

The first six verses of I John 4 contain a warning against false teachers. These are not easily detected, for they come as angels of light, but God sets forth a method whereby we can, without fail, detect whether or not a person is speaking according to the Spirit of God.

The first three verses say, "Beloved, believe not every spirit, but try the spirits whether they are of God: because many false prophets are gone out into the world. Hereby know ye the Spirit of God: Every spirit that confesseth that Jesus Christ is come in the flesh is of God: and every spirit that confesseth not that Jesus Christ is come in the flesh is not of God: and this is the spirit of antichrist, whereof ye have heard that it should come; and even now already is it in the world."

We are told to try the spirits. The word "try" means to prove or to test. We must try the spirits to see whether or not they are of God. We are instructed not to trust every spirit or every spiritual-sounding message.

Paul warned of the same danger when he wrote to the Corinthians: "For I am jealous over you with godly jealousy: for I have espoused you to one husband, that I may present you as a chaste virgin to Christ. But I fear, lest by any means, as the serpent beguiled Eve through his subtilty, so your minds should be corrupted from the simplicity that is in Christ. For if he that cometh preacheth another Jesus, whom we have not preached, or if ye receive another spirit, which ye have not received, or another gospel, which ye have not accepted, ye might well bear with him" (II Cor. 11:2-4).

Some may wonder about these words and ask if it is possible for someone to preach another Jesus. Yes, many have and many are doing so. There is the Jesus revealed in the Bible, and there is a man-made Jesus whom people have preached as a substitute for the real one. Paul went on to say, "For such are false apostles, deceitful workers, transforming themselves into the apostles of Christ. And no marvel; for Satan himself is transformed into an angel of light. Therefore it is no great thing if his ministers also be transformed as the ministers of righteousness; whose end shall be according to their works" (II Cor. 11:13-15).

Paul had to deal with the same situation when he wrote to the Galatian believers: "I marvel that ye are so soon removed from him that called you into the grace of Christ unto another gospel: which is not another; but there be some that trouble you, and would pervert the gospel of Christ. But though we, or an angel from heaven, preach any other gospel unto you than that which we have preached unto you, let him be accursed. As we said before, so say I now again, If any man preach any other gospel unto you than that ye have received, let him be accursed" (Gal. 1:6-9).

False teachers had taught the Galatian believers that they had to keep the Law with its various rituals if they would be saved. They taught another gospel, which was not the true gospel, and sought to remove the believers from Christ.

When the Apostle John said "try [prove] the spirits" (I John 4:1), he did not mean that we are to try them only once, for the tense of the verb used is the one frequently seen in this epistle. The meaning is "keep on trying the spirits." This, of course, does not mean that we are to try the same person or message again and again, but we are to test each person we hear by the principles given in this passage.

How to Test False Teachers

The method of testing is very simple. It is explained in these words: "Every spirit that confesseth that Jesus Christ is come in the flesh is of God" (I John 4:2). The subject here is not the Holy Spirit; it is either the spirit of man or some other being.

Such a spirit which is of God confesses that Jesus Christ is come in the flesh.

The name "Jesus" indicates His humanity. He was born of the virgin Mary, lived on this earth among men, was crucified, died and rose again the third day. The word "Jesus" means Saviour. Part of what a true spirit confesses is that Jesus is the Saviour.

But there is more to the test than this. The spirit which is of God is to confess that Jesus Christ is come in the flesh. "Christ" is the name which refers to the One anointed of God. It refers to the deity of the Saviour, the eternal Christ, by whom all things were created (see Col. 1:15-18). Consequently, if the spirit confesses that the eter-

71

nal God and Jesus, who died for our sins, are one, then that person knows the Lord.

We must believe that Jesus Christ is eternally God (see John 1:1). He is included in the name "Elohim" (God) of Genesis 1:1. He was from the beginning and still is a member of the triune God.

The Book of Hebrews says concerning Him, "[God] hath in these last days spoken unto us by his Son, whom he hath appointed heir of all things, by whom also he made the worlds; who being the brightness of his glory, and the express image of his person, and upholding all things by the word of his power, when he had by himself purged our sins, sat down on the right hand of the Majesty on high; being made so much better than the angels, as he hath by inheritance obtained a more excellent name than they. For unto which of the angels said he at any time, Thou art my Son, this day have I begotten thee? And again, I will be to him a Father, and he shall be to me a Son? And again, when he bringeth in the firstbegotten into the world, he saith, And let all the angels of God worship him.... And, Thou, Lord, in the beginning hast laid the foundation of the earth; and the heavens are the works of thine hands: they shall perish; but thou remainest; and they all shall wax old as doth a garment; and as a vesture shalt thou fold them up, and they shall be changed: but thou art the same, and thy years shall not fail" (1:2-6,10-12).

This One who made the world, who was and is the eternal God, was the Father's choice to become our Sin-Bearer: "We see Jesus, who was made a little lower than the angels for the suffering of death, crowned with glory and honour; that he by

72

the grace of God should taste death for every man"
(2:9).

The Situation Today

It is sad, but many who talk about our Saviour
and use His name do not believe that He is the
eternal God, the Creator of all things, and that He
came to die for the sins of mankind.

What He did by dying on the cross, being
buried and rising again from the dead is described
in I Corinthians 15:1-4. A person who believes
these facts is of God, according to the Scriptures.

On the other hand, John said that he who does
not confess that Jesus Christ came in the flesh is
not of God. I once read of a man who stated that it
was not important to him whether or not Jesus was
God. The thing that was important to him was how
Jesus lived. This man denied that Christ was come
in the flesh. None of us can be neutral on this
point. If a person does not affirm that Christ came
in the flesh, then by his very silence he is denying
Him.

The person who is of God will confess that
Jesus is the Christ, for the Holy Spirit is in him
and confirms it to him.

We have a great deal of imitation Christianity
today. People seek to pattern their lives after
Jesus. They use Him as an example, but that does
not make them real Christians, only synthetic ones.
It is not possible for an unsaved person to actually
pattern his life after Christ and to act like Him.

The genuine Christian is born spiritually of
God. The believer belongs to, or proceeds from,
God—we have Christ's life within. It is real, it is

true, it is pure, it is genuine, it is free from hypocrisy or pretense.

A Test for Genuine Salvation

How can this text we are considering be a sure proof of whether or not a person is born again?

There is a very real sense in which we are not to judge other people, but on the other hand we must know whether or not the message we listen to is the true gospel of Jesus Christ. We will have to account for the time and money spent in getting out the message that we are approving. The Scripture is not suggesting that we publicly blast a false teacher, but we must decide in our own hearts whether we care to bear the responsibility of helping to spread such a message.

This test is sure because the Holy Spirit is the only one who can reveal how God would come in the flesh. Paul said, "Wherefore I give you to understand, that no man speaking by the Spirit of God calleth Jesus accursed: and that no man can say that Jesus is the Lord, but by the Holy Ghost" (I Cor. 12:3). In another place he wrote: "But the natural man receiveth not the things of the Spirit of God: for they are foolishness unto him: neither can he know them, because they are spiritually discerned" (2:14). These great basic truths of the Christian faith are made plain only through the work of the Spirit of God. They are against all human reasoning and mere human understanding. There is no way of showing from the human perspective, either scientific or philosophical, how God could become man. But the Bible declares it, and by the Spirit we believe it.

On the other hand, people are foolish enough to teach evolution. They seek to show that a lower form of life can become a higher form. But they deny, or at least will not acknowledge, that God, who is life, could ever become man.

The spirit of man must be humbled before he will acknowledge these things. Human pride has to be thrust aside. There is no way the human intellect can explain these infinite truths. We simply accept them by faith.

There is a message here also for the child of God. There are degrees of spiritual growth, but no real progress will be made until the believer recognizes not only that Jesus Christ came in the flesh but also that He is Lord and Master. To repudiate or ignore either of these truths is to manifest the spirit of antichrist. There is a way of victory over this spirit of rebellion, however, and I John 4:4 indicates what that is.

The Overcomer

"Ye are of God, little children, and have overcome them: because greater is he that is in you, than he that is in the world" (I John 4:4). Today we need more overcomers. Potentially, every Christian is an overcomer. Actually, every Christian ought to be an overcomer.

The word "overcome" means "to gain the victory." When we have fought the battle, we will be victorious and will then be able to go on to greater triumphs. We face all types of enemies. That is why we are told, "Put on the whole armour of God, that ye may be able to stand against the wiles of the devil" (Eph. 6:11). The flesh (the old nature), the Devil, this whole world's system—all are against us. A fierce battle is raging. Satan would like us to go down to defeat instead of having the victory that Christ Jesus came to give us.

The formula for being overcomers is given in this section in I John. It is very simple. It is Christ in us, the hope of glory. "Greater is he that is in you, than he that is in the world" (4:4).

Light is shed on this subject in Romans 8: "For the law of the Spirit of life in Christ Jesus hath made me free from the law of sin and death" (v. 2). Later in this chapter Paul wrote: "What shall we then say to these things? If [since] God be for us, who can be against us? He that spared not his own Son, but delivered him up for us all, how shall he not with him also freely give us all things?" (vv. 31,32).

The same truth is taught in Galatians: "Are ye so foolish? Having begun in the Spirit, are ye now made perfect [mature] by the flesh?" (3:3). The answer, of course, is no. And in Galatians 5:16 we read: "Walk in the Spirit, and ye shall not fulfil the lust of the flesh." We are assured from these passages that victory is possible through Jesus Christ, who not only died for us but who also lives and is the new life in us.

Satan is strong, but Christ is stronger. Perhaps you have read the story of the little girl who said that sometimes Satan would knock at her door with a temptation, but she would say, "Jesus, will You please go and answer the door?" That was her childish way of stating a great truth. Satan can never stand against Christ, for Hebrews 2:14,15 tells us that when Jesus died, He broke the death-grip that Satan had on us.

How to Overcome

Fuller emphasis is given to this truth in I John 5: "For whatsoever is born of God overcometh the world: and this is the victory that overcometh the world, even our faith. Who is he that overcometh the world, but he that believeth that Jesus is the Son of God?" (vv. 4,5). Christ, the eternal Son of God, who came in the flesh, lived on the earth, was crucified, buried, rose again, is at the right hand of God and now lives in us, is the formula for victory. When trials come, remember this assurance. Victory has been provided for you; it is necessary only that you accept it.

The Children of Israel were instructed to cross the Jordan River at a time of flooding. There were no bridges or ferries, and the water was too deep to ford. But God promised that the moment the priests stepped into the water the waters would part. When the priests obeyed with the people following, the waters rolled back as God had promised, and the nation passed through on dry land.

This victory is like something that is kept in trust until needed and accepted. When the Israelites were told to take the city of Jericho, the task looked impossible. The city was surrounded by high and strong walls, but God assured His people that it was theirs. And it became theirs in actuality when they followed His instructions. Their faith enabled them to obey. They knew God would perform if they believed and obeyed.

Some of us hesitate to claim victory because we fail so often. Let us confess our failures to Him, and then believe that Jesus Christ in us is able to give victory. The words of admonition from Colossians are "As ye have therefore received Christ Jesus the Lord, so walk ye in him: rooted and built up in him, and stablished in the faith, as ye have been taught, abounding therein with thanksgiving" (2:6,7). The roots of a tree gather the life-giving moisture and food from the earth and send it up through the trunk into the branches and leaves. In this way the tree keeps growing and bearing fruit.

We are just like that. We have been planted in Jesus Christ. Our roots are there, and as we daily partake of the Word, meditate on it and assimilate it, our spiritual roots go deeper and deeper. We draw our strength, power and grace from the life that is in Christ.

In I John 4:5,6 John provided a test for salvation that must not be ignored: "They are of the world: therefore speak they of the world, and the world heareth them. We are of God: he that knoweth God heareth us; he that is not of God heareth not us. Hereby know we the spirit of truth, and the spirit of error."

In the verses previous to this the apostle discussed false teachers who talk about Jesus but fail to acknowledge that He truly is the Son of God. Such people are representatives of Satan, not messengers of God. They speak the type of message that the world loves to hear. Often based on human philosophy, it caters to the pride of intellect so prized by most people. Such teachers and those who delight in their teaching are unbelievers. Where, then, do you stand with reference to this matter? If you agree with them, then you, too, need to be born again.

On the other hand, how do I know that I am of God? I believe His Word. I believe that Jesus Christ is the eternal God, that He dwells in a glorified human body and that I shall be like Him, for one day I shall see Him as He is. I have no doubt about it. The people who are of God will accept this message, but those who are of the world will reject it. Classify yourself according to your attitude. It will let you know whether or not you are saved.

Paul wrote to Timothy: "Preach the word; be instant in season, out of season; reprove, rebuke, exhort with all longsuffering and doctrine. For the time will come when they will not endure sound doctrine; but after their own lusts shall they heap to themselves teachers, having itching ears; and they shall turn away their ears from the truth, and shall be turned unto fables" (II Tim. 4:2-4). The time that was future in Timothy's day we believe is now here. People are turning away from the truth and have itching ears. They do not want to hear what God has to say. They have gathered to themselves teachers who tell them the things they want to hear, even though those things are not true.

Love, the Motivating Force

"Beloved, let us love one another: for love is of God; and every one that loveth is born of God, and knoweth God. He that loveth not knoweth not God; for God is love. In this was manifested the love of God toward us, because that God sent his only begotten Son into the world, that we might live through him. Herein is love, not that we loved God, but that he loved us, and sent his Son to be the propitiation for our sins" (I John 4:7-10).

Love is the principle which governs and motivates the whole Christian life. The constraining

79

love of Christ (II Cor. 5:14) makes us want to do God's will, which, of course, includes living a godly Christian life. If such a motivating power is absent from our hearts, then we have good reason to question whether or not we are saved.

We are not suggesting that this love is perfected in the same way in all believers, for growth occurs in various stages. But we can test ourselves to see whether there is a desire to live for the Lord. Are we constantly wondering if we are going to get caught doing something wrong, or how we can get by with this or that? Such persons may be Christians, but they are living on a very low plane. If our Christian life is not motivated by love, then something is lacking.

In I Corinthians 13 we read: "Though I speak with the tongues of men and of angels, and have not charity [love], I am become as sounding brass, or a tinkling cymbal" (v. 1). Such ability to influence people amounts to nothing with God if love is not present. Verse 2 says, "And though I have the gift of prophecy, and understand all mysteries, and all knowledge; and though I have all faith, so that I could remove mountains, and have not charity [love], I am nothing."

Describing another group who had false ideas on this subject, Paul said, "And though I bestow all my goods to feed the poor, and though I give my body to be burned, and have not charity [love], it profiteth me nothing" (v. 3).

According to these verses, a believer may be very active in Christian service, but if love is not the motivating force in his life, he is missing the very thing that will bring him to spiritual maturity.

Releasing Love

There is an admonition in I John 4:7: "Let us love one another." The apostle did not say, "Try to create and produce love." He said, "Let us love." In other words, we are to release that love.

Some may protest and say they cannot love certain people. That is true from the natural standpoint, but we are not dealing with natural love. It is divine love, the love with which God loved us when we were unlovable and our sins had separated us from Him. Because he loved us God sent His Son to die for us. So we as believers are to love one another, for love is of God.

God, as to His nature, is love. And this love is shared with the believer. It has been shed abroad in the heart of each one (see Rom. 5:5). This love of God will grow within us and flow through us in an unbroken stream if we will let it. The Christian life, which is the power of the Holy Spirit within, is a life of love.

Any pool which does not have an outlet becomes stagnant. The love of God has been shed abroad in our hearts, but if it is only received and not permitted to flow out, we will become spiritually stagnant. The Dead Sea is so named because it has no outlet. Any lake whose waters are to remain fresh must have not only an inlet but also an outlet. And this is also true in the Christian life. One who only takes in and never gives out will cease to have the freshness of the Christ-life within. He will fail to help and encourage others.

Someone asked me this question: "How can you preach a sermon every day?" I said, "That's simple. God gives me a sermon, and I give it out and then have room for another one from Him." As we give out what we take in, we are able to keep on refreshing others through the ever-flowing love of God.

As we have already noted, the love of God can never be adequately seen unless we recognize it as expressed in Christ's sacrifice on Calvary. Christ, as the propitiation for our sins, is the greatest possible manifestation of the love of God for us. Jesus came here to die in order that we might be justified. God could not pass off sin lightly; its penalty had to be met and its power broken. And so Jesus came. This was not man seeking God but God seeking man.

The Suffering Saviour in Isaiah

Isaiah wrote about the suffering of Christ: "He is despised and rejected of men; a man of sorrows, and acquainted with grief: and we hid as it were our faces from him; he was despised, and we esteemed him not. Surely he hath borne our griefs, and carried our sorrows: yet we did esteem him stricken, smitten of God, and afflicted" (Isa. 53:3,4). He endured these things, but not for His own sins. He suffered and died as our substitute. "But he was wounded for our transgressions, he was bruised for our iniquities: the chastisement of our peace was upon him; and with his stripes we are healed. All we like sheep have gone astray; we have turned every one to his own way; and the Lord hath laid on him the iniquity of us all. He was oppressed, and he was afflicted, yet he opened not his mouth" (vv. 5-7).

82

The Suffering Saviour in the Psalms

In the Book of Hebrews we are told that there was a time when our Saviour offered up prayers and supplication with strong crying and tears (5:7). This may refer to His intense suffering on Calvary. This is described in part in Psalm 22: "I am poured out like water, and all my bones are out of joint: my heart is like wax; it is melted in the midst of my bowels. My strength is dried up like a potsherd; and my tongue cleaveth to my jaws; and thou hast brought me into the dust of death" (vv. 14,15). This is a description of death by crucifixion. He was nailed to the cross, it was raised into its place, and His body was racked with fierce pain as a result.

Men were astonished at His appearance, for He was so brutally treated that He hardly looked like a human being (Isa. 52:14). "There is no beauty that we should desire him" (53:2).

Psalm 22:1,2 says, "My God, my God, why hast thou forsaken me? Why art thou so far from helping me, and from the words of my roaring? O my God, I cry in the daytime, but thou hearest not; and in the night season, and am not silent." But His words were not a complaint. In the midst of His agony, He recognized why He was enduring it: "But thou art holy, O thou that inhabitest the praises of Israel. Our fathers trusted in thee: they trusted, and thou didst deliver them. They cried unto thee, and were delivered: they trusted in thee, and were not confounded. But I am a worm, and no man; a reproach of men, and despised of the people" (vv. 3-6).

83

In addition to physical suffering, our Saviour had to endure the scorn and the ridicule of the very men for whom He was dying. "All they that see me laugh me to scorn: they shoot out the lip, they shake the head, saying, He trusted on the Lord that he would deliver him: let him deliver him, seeing he delighted in him" (vv. 7,8).

Yes, God loved the world so much that He gave His only Son. He did not send an angel or some other messenger. He sent His only Son, the One in whom He delighted, the creator and heir of all things. Only He could redeem the souls of men.

We respond to God's love by trusting Christ and loving Him in return (see I John 4:19). Then God's love is shed abroad in our hearts through the Holy Spirit. Our love for God will be demonstrated by our love for other people. This, of course, involves more than just loving fellow believers. It means that our hearts will go out to a lost world just as God's heart did.

Love Proves God's Presence

God's love in us is the proof of His abiding presence, and His love manifested through us reveals God to others. "No man hath seen God at any time. If we love one another, God dwelleth in us, and his love is perfected in us" (I John 4:12). As this love is brought to maturity in us, others will see in us the life of God in the power of the Holy Spirit.

We cannot talk about being filled with the Holy Spirit if there are bitter criticisms in our hearts toward others. The love of God will enable us to judge righteously with regard to others, but bitter criticism, which is of the flesh and not of God, will not be manifested.

For example, Paul and Silas were unjustly beaten, thrown into prison and then placed in stocks overnight in Philippi (see Acts 16:12-34). If any men, humanly speaking, had reason to be resentful, it was these two preachers of the cross. But they were different, for Christ had changed their hearts, and they sang the praises of God so that other prisoners heard them. God sent an earthquake which shook the prison and released all the prisoners from the chains. The jailer, thinking the prisoners had escaped, threatened to take his own life. Paul was a man of love as well as a man of faith, and he called out to the jailer to do himself no harm because all the prisoners were present (vv. 25-29). No wonder the Philippian jailer cried out, "What must I do to be saved?" (v. 30).

During our Saviour's trial, Peter denied his Lord. After Peter had denied Jesus, "the Lord turned, and looked upon Peter" (Luke 22:61). It was a look of sorrow and a look of love, and that was all it took. Peter broke under it. He went out and wept bitterly (v. 62).

This love of God matures the Christian. I have seen many of God's people grow older in the Lord and grow more Christlike as they walked with Him from day to day. They took more time to be with the Lord and had their hearts filled with Him. Through this, their love was perfected toward others. This mature love expressed through God's people demonstrates to others that Christ lives in us.

Love in Operation

Repeated in I John 4:16 is the phrase "God is love." This introduces the subject of love in operation: "And we have known and believed the love that God hath to us. God is love; and he that dwelleth in love dwelleth in God, and God in him. Herein is our love made perfect, that we may have boldness in the day of judgment: because as he is, so are we in this world" (vv. 16,17).

Unbelievers know nothing of a God of love. Even in areas where there is so much preaching about the love of God, the very heart of the matter is ignored or denied through men who do not realize how God, in love, took care of the sin question. Sin is enmity against God. He could not tolerate it and could not live with it. It resulted in separation between us and God.

When God judged sin, whose penalty was death, the blow fell on His Son instead of on us. We were God's enemies; yet it was His Son who died for us, and it is this love which, in turn, motivates us.

A day of judgment is coming that only those who have the love of God in their hearts will be able to face with boldness. All people have an inner consciousness of this coming day, even though many of them try to hide it.

Perfect Love Casts Out Fear

To the person who has received the love of God and found life in Christ, that day of judgment holds no fear. We will not face an angry judge, for the penalty for our sins has already been paid by Christ. He will welcome us in love, not in anger.

"There is no fear in love; but perfect love casteth out fear: because fear hath torment. He that feareth is not made perfect in love" (I John 4:18). Love removes the dread of that coming day of wrath. But to the person who has not availed himself of salvation in Christ, thought of that day brings fear. The physical torment will not be the hardest thing to endure. That torment of mind and heart, resulting from the fact that the only way of salvation was rejected, will cause unending grief.

Believers can rejoice in these reassuring words: "What shall we then say to these things? If God be for us, who can be against us? He that spared not his own Son, but delivered him up for us all, how shall he not with him also freely give us all things? Who shall lay anything to the charge of God's elect? It is God that justifieth. Who is he that condemneth? It is Christ that died, yea rather, that is risen again, who is even at the right hand of God, who also maketh intercession for us. Who shall separate us from the love of Christ? Shall tribulation, or distress, or persecution, or famine, or nakedness, or peril, or sword? As it is written, For thy sake we are killed all the day long; we are accounted as sheep for the slaughter. Nay, in all these things we are more than conquerors through him that loved us. For I am persuaded, that neither death, nor life, nor angels, nor principalities, nor powers, nor things present, nor things to come, nor height, nor depth, nor any other creature, shall be able to separate us from the love of God, which is in Christ Jesus our Lord" (Rom. 8:31-39).

The last two verses of I John 4 say, "If a man

say, I love God, and hateth his brother, he is a liar: for he that loveth not his brother whom he hath seen, how can he love God whom he hath not seen? And this commandment have we from him, That he who loveth God love his brother also."

The love that we have for God is measured by the love that we have for other people. The closer we walk with God, the sweeter will be our love for others. Here is a good test: Select someone who is seemingly unlovable. Ask yourself, How can I get along with that person? How can I show my love to him?

We may disagree with the person over issues or principles, but that need not affect our love for him or her. It is not necessary that we agree on all points with another person before we can love him. In fact, it is a greater expression of the life of Christ within us to show kindness and consideration to those with whom we disagree on certain things. This can indeed be a real test of our love for God. Our love for other people will prove how much we love the Saviour. Seek to love the unlovable; this is the acid test of our love for God.

Chapter 5

Additional Truth on the Overcomer

The first three verses of I John 5 are a review: "Whosoever believeth that Jesus is the Christ is born of God: and every one that loveth him that begat loveth him also that is begotten of him. By this we know that we love the children of God, when we love God, and keep his commandments. For this is the love of God, that we keep his commandments: and his commandments are not grievous."

This is repetition for emphasis, but an additional thought is added in the expression "his commandments are not grievous." The Saviour Himself declared, "My yoke is easy, and my burden is light" (Matt. 11:30). That which would be an impossibility for an unbeliever and an irksome task for the carnal Christian is a delight to the one who surrenders his all to Christ.

Verses 4 and 5 of I John 5 are very important to believers: "For whosoever is born of God overcometh the world: and this is the victory that overcometh the world, even our faith. Who is he that overcometh the world, but he that believeth that Jesus is the Son of God?" This theme was discussed in our study of Chapter 4, but further study may be helpful. Many of the letters that reach the Back to the Bible Broadcast are concerned with this very subject.

You will recall that we have already pointed out that the Christian is engaged in a great battle. For that reason we are to put on the whole armor of God (see Eph. 6:11-13). The battle is described in verse 12: "For we wrestle not against flesh and blood, but against principalities, against powers, against the rulers of the darkness of this world, against spiritual wickedness in high places."

The Christian is harassed on every side by evil forces. The world system, which God says is controlled by the Evil One, is against us. We have a foe in the form of the old nature, which is within us. And, of course, the Devil is against us.

We seem to be living in a time when these evil forces are accentuated to an extreme. So-called paganism is no longer confined to areas of the world considered to be uncivilized.

In spite of the fact that we are surrounded by all this evil, we are assured by Ephesians 6:3 that by putting on the whole armor of God we can stand in the evil day. We will be victorious, in other words. When the fight is over, we will stand as victors.

Why Such a Battle?

Perhaps some wonder why we should enter such a battle. Why doesn't God end this conflict once and for all? There is both a negative and a positive side to the answer.

The negative side is that Satan, through the flesh or the world or evil spirits, will try to ruin our Christian life and testimony. Before we were saved we were of no great concern to the Evil One, for

90

we were following along with the world system. But when we try to live for the Lord, we find that Satan opposes us. We must enter the battle to overcome Satan's attacks.

On the positive side is the fact that by entering into this warfare and overcoming, glory is brought to the name of Christ. Our sole purpose for being here is to glorify Him. Except for that, God would have taken us right to heaven as soon as we trusted Christ as Saviour. Having decided to leave us here to fight in this warfare, God has assured us that by utilizing the powers and weapons provided for us we can be victorious.

Overcoming should increasingly become the habit of the Christian life. "For whatsoever is born of God overcometh the world" (I John 5:4).

How to Win

The method of victory is by employing faith. "And this is the victory that overcometh the world, even our faith" (I John 5:4).

An illustration from Israel's experience helps us understand this. When God spoke to Joshua concerning the Promised Land, He said, "Every place that the sole of your foot shall tread upon, that have I given unto you" (Josh. 1:3). It was really theirs, but they had to take possession of it, or appropriate it. They stepped out in faith, anticipating that when they reached that land, they would conquer it. But they came to the Jordan River, which was a great barrier. It looked at first like an insurmountable one, but when they obeyed God and the priests stepped into the water, the waters parted, and the Children of Israel walked across on dry ground.

The victory over Satan has already been won for us through Christ, but we must appropriate that victory daily in faith.

We are told what it is that faith believes: "Who is he that overcometh the world, but he that believeth that Jesus is the Son of God?" (I John 5:5). When we really grasp the truth that Jesus, who lives in us, is God and wants to use His great power in and through us, we will no longer have difficulty claiming spiritual victory.

Difference Between Knowing and Believing

What is the difference between knowing the fact that Jesus Christ is the eternal Son of God and believing it? We can know things from the historical standpoint, and yet that knowledge does not necessarily affect our conduct.

Believing, as used in this context, means more than mere mental assent. It also carries the thought of living in accordance with what we know. How we can do that as Christians is evident from the Scriptures. For example, a passage in Colossians says, "As ye have therefore received Christ Jesus the Lord, so walk ye in him" (2:6). Notice that little word "as." We receive Jesus not only as Saviour but also as our Lord, meaning that He should have full control of our lives. But it means more than that. It means that He is our life (see 3:4). So to believe that Jesus Christ is God means more than just mental assent to that fact. It also involves the fact that He lives within us.

Walking in Christ

What does it mean to walk in Him? The answer is given in Ephesians 6:10: "Finally, my brethren, be strong in the Lord, and in the power of his might." We are not told here to receive strength from the Lord. Our capacity for strength is limited, and even if filled to that capacity, we would still be very weak. Our strength is the Lord Himself.

We are members of the Body of Jesus Christ just as our limbs are members of our physical bodies. My hand, for example, does its work in the strength of the life that I possess. It cannot function apart from me. But as part of my body it lives and functions in my strength. So it is with us who are members of Christ's Body. His life flows in and through us.

Consequently, we should not pray, "Please give us strength today." Instead, we should recognize that as members of the Body of Christ, He is our strength. We fight the enemy through Christ, who lives in us.

Colossians 2:7 states, "Rooted and built up in him, and stablished in the faith, as ye have been taught, abounding therein with thanksgiving." As we have received the Saviour, we are to go on living in Him. We are to grow out of Him as a plant grows out of the soil in which it is planted. We are rooted in Him; we are part of Him. As we grow, our lives will overflow with joy and thankfulness.

A grave warning is given in Colossians 2:8: "Beware lest any man spoil you through philosophy and vain deceit, after the tradition of men, after the rudiments of the world, and not after Christ." We are to be careful that no one spoils our faith through some intellectual or high-sounding non-sense. We are not to let human ideas spoil our Christian lives. Our life is in Christ. "For in him dwelleth all the fulness of the Godhead bodily. And ye are complete in him, which is the head of all principality and power" (vv. 9,10). He is our head, and through Him comes all power and strength so that we have all the resources for victory in the day of battle. We can see from all of this that to believe that Jesus is the Son of God is a matter of tremendous importance.

Spiritual Circumcision

"In whom also ye are circumcised with the circumcision made without hands, in putting off the body of the sins of the flesh by the circumcision of Christ" (Col. 2:11). The circumcision that the Israelites practiced was a physical act, but God says that our circumcision is that of the Spirit by Jesus Christ, which sets us free from sin. In His death Christ died to sin and broke its power. If I, therefore, trust in Him and live a life of faith in Him, I will be set free from the power of sin. This is the same truth presented in I John.

Christ the Head of the Body

"And not holding the Head, from which all the body by joints and bands having nourishment ministered, and knit together, increaseth with the increase of God" (Col. 2:19). The New American Standard Bible translates this verse as follows: "And not holding fast to the head, from whom the entire body, being supplied and held together by

94

the joints and ligaments, grows with a growth which is from God." Jesus is compared to the physical head. From the head through the joints, the nervous system, the digestive and circulatory systems and so on, the physical body is nourished. So spiritually we are nourished through Christ.

This leads us to a very important conclusion. We cannot continue to have victory in our lives if we do not take the necessary nourishment. There must be a daily appropriation through faith if we are to victoriously live the new life in Christ. We cannot ignore Colossians 3:16,17: "Let the word of Christ dwell in you richly in all wisdom; teaching and admonishing one another in psalms and hymns and spiritual songs, singing with grace in your hearts to the Lord. And whatsoever ye do in word or deed, do all in the name of the Lord Jesus, giving thanks to God and the Father by him." The battle is a daily one, and the victory must also be daily. We must settle each day who is going to rule in our lives. Give the Lord that place moment by moment and feed constantly on His Word.

Another scripture which helps us in this warfare is Luke 9:23: "And he said to them all, If any man will come after me, let him deny himself, and take up his cross daily, and follow me." To follow Him is to be assured of victory, but several things are involved here. We must deny ourselves, that is, disown ourselves, and recognize that we do not have a right to ourselves or the strength with which to fight successfully. We must also take up the cross daily, which means that we must recognize we have died to sin and then follow the Saviour. In doing this, we decide who is to be boss for the day.

From our leader we receive our orders. (See Rom. 6:11-13.)

Remember, this is a daily matter. When we fail, we should acknowledge the failure (I John 1:9), thank God for forgiveness and appropriate the strength again. Do this every time you fail.

Getting into the Word

We find His mind in the Word that He has given us. As that Word lights our path and shows the sin in our lives, we must confess that sin and failure to Him. He will forgive us, and we will be ready to go on again. But we must constantly get into His Word.

The psalmist said, "Thy word have I hid in mine heart, that I might not sin against thee" (Ps. 119:11). This calls for meditating on the Word and not merely reading it. To read it is good and commendable, but to take time to meditate on it is excellent. Study each separate word and phrase carefully, and let God speak to your heart through it.

The psalmist said in another place, "But his delight is in the law of the Lord; and in his law doth he meditate day and night" (1:2). Commit that Word to memory and then meditate on it in your heart. In the waking hours of the night let God speak to your heart through it. By this we will make our way prosperous and successful in the sight of God.

Psalm 1 shows us that the person who is constantly dwelling in the Word is "like a tree planted by the rivers of water, that bringeth forth his fruit in his season; his leaf also shall not wither; and whatsoever he doeth shall prosper" (v. 3). A tree planted by the rivers of water cannot dry up. It will bear its fruit in season. That does not mean that a tree bears fruit all the time, but it bears fruit when it should. This will be the case with us if we consistently study and meditate on God's Word.

People do not overcome because they do not study the Word. But when God's people read His Word, meditate on it and act on it, they will overcome.

Once during a series of meetings, dozens of people spoke to me about their spiritual difficulties. Each problem was different but in each case the first question I asked was, Have you taken proper time each morning to meditate alone in the Word of God? In every case the people admitted that they had not. That was the key to their difficulty. God will work for us, in us and through us when we follow the path He has prescribed for us in His Word.

Most of us will never find time to meditate on the Word until we take that time, and take it we must if we want to prosper in the things of God. The best time to take it is in the early morning, before the day's rush and problems begin.

A Basis for Assurance

The verses we are now going to consider form a climax to the Book of First John. "He that believeth on the Son of God hath the witness in himself: he that believeth not God hath made him a liar; because he believeth not the record that God gave of his Son. And this is the record, that God hath given to us eternal life, and this life is in his Son.

He that hath the Son hath life; and he that hath not the Son of God hath not life. These things have I written unto you that believe on the name of the Son of God" (I John 5:10-13).

The fact that people are dead in trespasses and sins is taken for granted in these verses. That "the wages of sin is death" (Rom. 6:23) is the background for these statements concerning life in Christ. This is in keeping with Ephesians 2:1-3: "And you hath he quickened, who were dead in trespasses and sins: wherein in time past ye walked according to the course of this world, according to the prince of the power of the air, the spirit that now worketh in the children of disobedience: among whom also we all had our conversation in times past in the lusts of our flesh, fulfilling the desires of the flesh and of the mind; and were by nature the children of wrath, even as others."

God did not leave us in that condition however. "But God, who is rich in mercy, for his great love wherewith he loved us, even when we were dead in sins, hath quickened us together with Christ, (by grace ye are saved)" (vv. 4,5).

Life Is in the Son

"This is the record, that God hath given to us eternal life, and this life is in his Son" (I John 5:11). The person who has the Son has life, and the one who does not have the Son of God does not have life. The life spoken of in I John is eternal life.

God has proved through various tests over the course of history that man cannot attain to life, retain life when it is given him or produce life. Man was given life from the creative hand of God, but the period of innocence proved that he could not retain life. Then under the Dispensation of Conscience it became evident that man could not produce spiritual life. Under the Law, God proved that works could not produce this life; it is a gift from God. God alone can produce life, and He alone can keep that life. Once we realize that truth, we can begin growing in the Spirit.

This whole Book of I John centers around the fact that life is in the Son of God and that whoever has the Son has life.

Our earthly lifespan is very brief. The soul is eternal; that is, it has eternal existence, but eternal existence is not eternal life. God is the source of eternal life, and people receive it only through the method that God has planned. If God were to give us this eternal life in the sense that He gave life to Adam and Eve, we would forfeit it. We could not retain it. It is not given to us in that sense. This may sound contradictory, but this is what we mean: We are given this life as we are united with Jesus Christ. This is not a possession we receive apart from God. But we are made a part of this life by becoming one with Christ.

Perhaps an illustration will help to clarify this point. My foot has life because it is a part of my body. Apart from my body it would have no life, but joined with my body it has the life of the body.

Christ produces spiritual life in us and also sustains this life for us. In his Gospel, John wrote: "In the beginning was the Word, and the Word was with God, and the Word was God. The same was in the beginning with God. All things were made by

99

him; and without him was not any thing made that was made" (1:1-3). Christ, then, is Creator not only in the physical realm but also in the spiritual realm. Verse 4 says, "In him was life; and the life was the light of men." Later on we read: "And the Word was made flesh, and dwelt among us" (v. 14).

"He came unto his own, and his own received him not. But as many as received him, to them gave he power to become the sons of God, even to them that believe on his name: which were born, not of blood, nor of the will of the flesh, nor of the will of man, but of God" (vv. 11-13). By receiving Christ we enter into this life. He produces this life in us by the new birth, a spiritual birth. To those who receive Him, He gives the power, the very life itself, to become the sons of God. Verse 13 emphasizes the fact that people are not the source of this life; it comes from God alone.

"For by grace are ye saved through faith; and that not of yourselves: it is the gift of God: not of works, lest any man should boast. For we are his workmanship, created in Christ Jesus unto good works, which God hath before ordained that we should walk in them" (Eph. 2:8-10). Salvation is of God. Even saving faith comes from Him. Recognizing, then, that as sinners we were dead in trespasses and sins, that God offered us life in Christ and that we accepted it, we now have a basis for assurance. That is why John said, "These things have I written unto you that believe on the name of the Son of God; that ye may know that ye have eternal life" (I John 5:13).

Even the repetitions in this little book are not without great significance. Notice that in verse 13 the phrase "believe on the name of the Son of

100

God" is stated twice. Why? The faith whereby we are saved is also the faith by which we live. First, we believe on the name of Christ for salvation, and then we keep on believing in that name in order to live godly lives.

Verses 14 and 15 repeat a truth concerning prayer that has been considered before. "And this is the confidence that we have in him, that, if we ask any thing according to his will, he heareth us: and if we know that he hear us, whatsoever we ask, we know that we have the petitions that we desired of him." This certainly obligates us to continuously study the Bible. We must get alone with God to know His will as found in His Word. If we ask according to His will, we know that we have the answer to our petition.

The Sin unto Death

The next section in I John 5 deals with intercessory prayer and the restoration of a believer who has sinned: "If any man see his brother sin a sin which is not unto death, he shall ask, and he shall give him life for them that sin not unto death. There is a sin unto death: I do not say that he shall pray for it. All unrighteousness is sin: and there is a sin not unto death" (vv. 16,17). Two kinds of sin are mentioned here—one for which there can be restoration and a "sin unto death."

The word "brother" is used here, which would indicate that believers are being referred to and not unsaved persons. So we understand that the "sin unto death" is something committed by believers. Consider the believer who sins a sin not unto death and the matter of his restoration. We are to pray for him. Further light is shed on this in Paul's letter to the Galatians: "Brethren, if a man be overtaken in a fault, ye which are spiritual, restore such an one in the spirit of meekness; considering thyself, lest thou also be tempted" (6:1).

When a Christian is overtaken in a fault, the spiritual Christian is to restore him. We must understand the word "spiritual" in light of the Scriptures. "If we live in the Spirit, let us also walk in the Spirit" (5:25). A spiritual person recognizes that he himself has no life, that he cannot produce spiritual life, but that the Holy Spirit lives within him and forms the Christ-life within him. Only a person of that attitude of mind and heart can fulfill the responsibility of the Scriptures.

A warning is given to the spiritual Christian to seek to restore the erring brother in a spirit of meekness. Spiritual Christians may be overtaken in faults too. Consequently, they must be careful of their own attitude.

The restoration may be realized through conversation and prayer with the one at fault, or prayer alone may be all that is necessary.

With regard to the brother who sins unto death, John's words seem rather peculiar. "I do not say that he shall pray for it" (I John 5:16). We do not always know whether a Christian's sin is unto death; for that reason my own suggestion is that we should be sure to pray for such a person if we are in doubt. If we see that God is not going to answer, it could be that the person prayed for has committed a sin unto death. But I will continue to pray for such a person until the Spirit in some way makes it plain just what has happened in his life.

Distinction Between Unpardonable Sin and Sin unto Death

We, of course, want to know what this sin unto death is. First, however, there is in my mind a distinction between a sin unto death and the sin against the Holy Spirit. The two are not the same sin; yet there is a similarity.

The sin against the Holy Spirit, commonly known as the unpardonable sin, is the willful sin of an unbeliever. It is described in Matthew 12:22-32, where Jesus accused the scribes and Pharisees of having committed, or of at least being in danger of committing, this sin. It is a deliberate sin, one against better knowledge. When the Holy Spirit has convicted a person and he turns against the light he has received, in the sense that the Pharisees did, then he commits this sin. The Saviour said to the Pharisees, "Search the scriptures; for in them ye think ye have eternal life: and they are they which testify of me" (John 5:39). Then He added: "Ye will not come to me, that ye might have life" (v. 40). They wanted the honor of men and chose that rather than eternal life. They had been convicted by the Scriptures, by the Holy Spirit and by the life of Jesus Christ, but they deliberately turned away from Him to their own ways.

They also accused Him of casting out demons by the power of Beelzebub. That was the result of their having committed the sin against the Holy Spirit. This was a willful, planned sin on the part of these unbelieving yet religious people. Have you ever noticed that after Jesus spoke thus to the scribes and Pharisees, He always spoke to the rest of the people in parables? The Holy Spirit would

103

interpret the parables to those who were seeking the truth, and those who had rejected Him would not understand it.

The sin unto death is also a willful sin in that it is deliberately going against the will of the Holy Spirit. It is not the sin of an unbeliever but is instead the willful sin of a believer.

The same thought is expressed in Hebrews 10, which was written to Israelites who had come to know the Lord and were in danger of turning against Him. "For if we sin wilfully after that we have received the knowledge of the truth, there remaineth no more sacrifice for sins, but a certain fearful looking for of judgment and fiery indignation, which shall devour the adversaries" (vv. 26,27). Here the willful sin of a believer who knows the truth is described. In the case of these Hebrew Christians, they possibly did not want to undergo further persecution and decided to turn their backs on the truth concerning Christ. They were not willing to go on and mature, and their rebellion was a sin unto death.

The psalmist said, "Keep back thy servant also from presumptuous sins; let them not have dominion over me" (Ps. 19:13).

Sin unto Death Defined

I believe that the sin unto death is a deliberate sin of a believer against better knowledge. When John wrote about committing this sin, he used the tense so often employed throughout his first epistle, the tense which signifies continuation of action. In my opinion the sin unto death is a deliberately planned and willful persistence in some evil

104

course with the guilty person presuming on God's grace or mercy.

There may be those who have said, "Since I am eternally saved, I can live just as I please." They willfully and deliberately ignore the new life within them and its urging to godly living. I believe such a person stands in danger of committing the sin unto death.

The death which results from this sin, as far as I can determine from Scripture, is physical death, not spiritual death. There is a vast difference between the two.

John 5:24 says, "Verily, verily, I say unto you, He that heareth my word, and believeth on him that sent me, hath everlasting life, and shall not come into condemnation; but is passed from death unto life." How can that man fall back into death since he has already passed out of death into life? He was dead in trespasses and sins but has been resurrected.

The death spoken of in John 5:24 is spiritual death. The person who trusts in Christ for salvation will not come into the condemnation involving spiritual death because Christ has already borne that, and God cannot turn His back on the finished work of His Son. In Hebrews 10:10 we read: "By the which will we are sanctified through the offering of the body of Jesus Christ once for all." In verses 17 and 18 are these words: "And their sins and iniquities will I remember no more. Now where remission of these is, there is no more offering for sin." In other words, another offering is not provided since Christ has accomplished this death once and for all. But to continue in willful sin will bring the believer into (premature) physical death.

105

Sin Unto Death Illustrated From Scripture

A strong illustration of the sin unto death is found in I Corinthians 5:1-5. Here Paul was writing to the Corinthians about a man who was living in deliberately planned and willful sin. Paul denounced this man and instructed the Corinthians on how to handle this matter: "Deliver such an one unto Satan [excommunicate him from your church and deliver him over to Satan] for the destruction of the flesh [the body], that the spirit may be saved in the day of the Lord Jesus [resurrection day]" (v. 5). Physical death was the judgment stipulated in this case.

Joab's slaying of Abner was a willful, deliberately planned sin. This sin was punished by death. When David was dying, he reminded Solomon, who was to be the new king, of what Joab did and decreed that Solomon must deal with him. Joab tried to plead innocent and hung onto the horns of the altar, but to no avail. He was executed because he had committed a deliberate sin (II Sam. 3; I Kings 2).

David committed a deliberate sin, and when faced with it, he confessed it (II Sam. 12:13,14). He expected to die, for it was a deliberate sin. The prophet told David that he would not die but that his son would. This was a case of substitutionary death—an innocent one bore the penalty for the guilty one.

In Psalm 51, where David expressed his grief and repentance following this great sin, he cried: "For thou desirest not sacrifice; else would I give it: thou delightest not in burnt-offering. The sacrifices of God are a broken spirit: a broken and a

106

contrite heart, O God, thou wilt not despise" (vv. 16,17). So God spared the life of David, but his son bore the penalty.

Other similar instances—Israel at Kadesh-barnea, Achan at Jericho, Saul as king—all illustrate this particular sin unto death.

In the New Testament, even though God provided salvation for sinners so that through faith in Christ they passed from death to life, He used physical judgment as a means of discipline. Forgiveness was provided by confession. "If we confess our sins, he is faithful and just to forgive us our sins" (I John 1:9). But willful sin will bring the judgment of God.

Hebrews 10:26 states, "For if we [continuously] sin wilfully after that we have received the knowledge of the truth, there remaineth no more sacrifice for sins." There was a "fearful looking for of judgment and fiery indignation, which shall devour the adversaries" (v. 27). In other words, there was a waiting for God's judgment on the flesh because of the terrible sin.

This judgment is also mentioned in I Corinthians 3:17: "If any man defile the temple of God [the believer's body], him shall God destroy." The apostle was speaking of a deliberate defiling of the body, in full knowledge that the Holy Spirit indwells the believer.

In I Corinthians 11 this subject is clearly mentioned again. The particular sin in question was participation in the Lord's Table in an unworthy manner, growing out of a deliberate sin against better knowledge. "But let a man examine himself, and so let him eat of that bread, and drink of that cup. For he that eateth and drinketh unworthily,

107

eateth and drinketh damnation to himself, not dis-
cerning the Lord's body. For this cause many are
weak and sickly among you and many sleep"
(vv. 28-30). Paul was, no doubt, referring to the
physical sleep of death. Some of the Corinthian
believers had died suddenly, and others were sick,
apparently marked for death. Then he said that if
we would judge ourselves, we should not be judged
by Him (v. 31). But when we are chastened by
Him, it is so that we will not be condemned at the
end of the age (v. 32).

The sin unto death is one committed by a child
of God who deliberately presumes on God's grace.
God says that He will punish such a person in the
body so that he will not continue to add to that
sin. Remember also that believers will have to meet
Him at the Judgment Seat of Christ (see II Cor.
5:10).

Conclusion

The last few verses of I John 5 are basically
restatements of truth already covered in the body
of the epistle. In verse 18 the apostle restated the
whole matter of sanctification. In verse 19 he restated the truth concerning regeneration. And in
verse 20 he restated the truth about the Incarnation. We might have put these truths in the reverse
order, for the Incarnation came first in time. Christ
had to become man in order to provide a means of
salvation through regeneration. Then through His
living in us He provides sanctification. God, however, must have had some good reason for using the

order He did. It is surely significant that the Incarnation is the last subject as well as the first to appear in this brief letter.

The Christian's Attitude Toward False Teachers

In I John we learned the answer to two questions: What is a Christian? What constitutes Christianity? Though brief, II John is also very important. From it the Christian can learn what his attitude toward false teachers should be. Possibly at no other time in the history of the Church have there been so many religious leaders pretending to follow the Scriptures. In reality, they are mortal enemies of the Bible and of Christ.

The discussion of this subject begins with verse 7 of II John: "For many deceivers are entered into the world, who confess not that Jesus Christ is come in the flesh. This is a deceiver and an antichrist. Look to yourselves, that we lose not those things which we have wrought, but that we receive a full reward. Whosoever transgresseth, and abideth not in the doctrine of Christ, hath not God. He that abideth in the doctrine of Christ, he hath both the Father and the Son. If there come any unto you, and bring not this doctrine, receive him not into your house, neither bid him God speed: for he that biddeth him God speed is partaker of his evil deeds" (vv. 7-11).

111

A Balanced View Needed

In this passage we have a very important message for our day. I believe some add to what John says here, but others do not see this truth at all. Neither position is justified. There is a negative and a positive side to the truth given here. Some persons classify anything that does not agree with their denominational teaching or their particular slant on doctrine as being from false teachers. But God clarifies the real issues for us, pointing out who the false teachers are and what we are to do with regard to their support. He shows us what our attitude toward them should be.

The first clarification is given in verse 3: "Grace be with you, mercy, and peace, from God the Father, and from the Lord Jesus Christ, the Son of the Father, in truth and love." In other words, this verse tells us that we are to live and act in the sphere of truth and love. They go together. We are not to be guilty of emphasizing truth to the exclusion of love, nor are we to emphasize love to the neglect of truth. Both truth and love are needed. We are to speak "the truth in love" (Eph. 4:15).

Some persons tell us that we should not separate from anyone in Protestant groups on the basis of doctrine, that to do so shows a lack of love. But this could lead to a denial of the truth itself, as our study will show. John makes it plain that such a separation must be made when basic doctrines of the faith are denied.

Love

In verses 4-6 of II John, God tells us something about the kind of love in which He wants us to walk: "I rejoiced greatly that I found of thy children walking in truth, as we have received a commandment from the Father. And now I beseech thee, lady, not as though I wrote a new commandment unto thee, but that which we had from the beginning, that we love one another. And this is love, that we walk after his commandments. This is the commandment, That, as ye have heard from the beginning, ye should walk in it."

This love is not filial love, which means to have affection for someone as a friend. I can love persons in that sense, and yet fall far short of loving them in the spiritual manner intended. The love of which the apostle spoke is demonstrated through a determination of the will to do good to others regardless of their response to you. All the commandments of the Old and New Testaments are wrapped up in that one word—love. If I love my brother in this way, I will do him good, not harm.

Truth

To whom are we to give this kind of love? Who am I to support materially and spiritually? Who am I to bid Godspeed? We need to understand what is meant by "truth." We may vary among ourselves with regard to details of doctrine, but what is basic, or foundational, to our faith? God gives us this knowledge in this passage so that we can clearly differentiate between those who are preaching the truth and those who are not.

John declared that many deceivers have entered into the world and then stated who they are. They are those "who confess not that Jesus Christ is come in the flesh. This is a deceiver and an antichrist" (II John 1:7). That statement is short, but there is a great deal to it—more than appears on the surface.

Consider a passage in I John, where the same subject was dealt with: "Little children, it is the last time: and as ye have heard that antichrist shall come, even now are there many antichrists; whereby we know that it is the last time. They went out from us, but they were not of us; for if they had been of us, they would no doubt have continued with us: but they went out, that they might be made manifest that they were not all of us" (2:18,19).

Antichrists Identified

The first identifying mark of those who are called "antichrists" is that they left the fellowship of God's children. The second identifying mark is given in II John, where we learn that they denied the incarnation of the Lord Jesus Christ. The word "incarnation" means that the Lord Jesus Christ—who is eternally God, the Jehovah of the Old Testament, the Creator of the universe—came in the flesh. He was the Jesus who walked on the earth for 33 years, the One who became flesh and blood. He died for us, was buried, rose again from the dead and is now at the right hand of the Father. In other words, the man Christ Jesus is the eternal God. The "antichrists" of John's day denied this fact.

Some today deny that Jesus is a member of the Godhead. To them He is a Jesus other than the One presented in the New Testament. To them, He is a great man, the greatest of all teachers, but not the eternal Son of God. God called such teachers antichrists. "Hereby know ye the Spirit of God: Every spirit that confesseth that Jesus Christ is come in the flesh is of God: and every spirit that confesseth not that Jesus Christ is come in the flesh is not of God: and this is that spirit of antichrist, whereof ye have heard that it should come; and even now already is it in the world" (I John 4:2,3).

Some approach the subject from another angle but reach the same conclusion. They teach that Jesus Christ was the first being of God's creation. But they also deny the truth and are antichrists, for Jesus was not the first being of God's creation; He was the Creator.

Many others claim that the mother of Jesus is "the mother of God." By saying this, they place Jesus below a woman—a good woman, but still an earthly woman. Therefore, they deny that Jesus was eternally God. In their theologies they state that He is the second Person in the Trinity, but the logical impact of their teaching concerning Mary is to exalt her above Christ so that she replaces Him in God's scheme of redemption.

Another religious movement of our day, which states its belief in the deity of Christ, has much to say concerning salvation by grace through faith. Yet these people include a very subtle requirement of keeping the Law for salvation. In effect, this movement strikes at the heart of the work of Christ by denying its efficacy. Basic Christian truth

115

is denied in many ways today, and we must be alert and spiritually awake to detect such movements.

Disagreements Among Believers

Among persons who believe the Bible, some may not agree on some phases of doctrine, such as details relating to the Second Coming of Christ. They may not agree concerning some minor aspects of baptism or even of church government, but if they believe that Jesus Christ is eternally God, if they are born of God, if they preach the gospel, they are members of God's family. They will give evidence of knowing and doing the true work of every Christian, which is to make known that Jesus Christ came to save sinners (John 6:29,35,47).

Only by the Spirit of God can we say that Jesus Christ is a member of the Godhead and came in the flesh. Proof of this is found in I Corinthians 12:3: "Wherefore I give you to understand, that no man speaking by the Spirit of God calleth Jesus accursed: and that no man can say that Jesus is the Lord, but by the Holy Ghost." When a person honestly admits that Jesus Christ is eternally God and is the Lord of his life, he is born of God.

So we must distinguish between false teachers and those who are not, even if the true teachers do not agree on some points of doctrine. Not everyone with whom we disagree is an antichrist, though some of us are guilty of labeling them as such. The marks of the anti-Christian spirit have been clearly pointed out so that we should have no difficulty in recognizing false teachers. God wants us to bid

Godspeed to those who are His true children and are teaching the truth, but He tells us that we are not to have anything to do with those who are antichrists. We are not even to wish them Godspeed.

Whom Should the Christian Support?

In our study in II John, we discovered the identity of the false teachers and learned that we were not even to wish them Godspeed. To do so would be to ally ourselves with them, to join in their evil teaching.

We saw that these antichrists were those who denied that Jesus Christ is God. They denied that He came to this earth in a human body, lived for 33 years among men, died for their sins on Calvary and rose again from the dead. By rejecting these truths, these false teachers denied everything that pertains to our salvation. They denied all the truths that are basic to the Christian faith.

Christ Is Unique

A very sad fact is that many Christians are themselves not well informed concerning Christ. They do not seem to know that Jesus was and is unique. There never was another person like Him, and there never will be. He has always existed, for the Bible tells us, "In the beginning was the Word, and the Word was with God, and the Word was God. The same was in the beginning with God" (John 1:1,2).

Some will immediately protest that this passage is not talking about Jesus Christ but about "the

119

Word." Before answering that, let us see what this passage says concerning "the Word." "All things were made by him; and without him was not any thing made that was made. In him was life; and the life was the light of men. And the light shineth in darkness; and the darkness comprehended it not" (vv. 3-5). The Apostle John was obviously referring to a Person in these verses. That this Person was seen in the form of a human being is expressed in verse 14: "And the Word was made flesh, and dwelt among us, (and we beheld his glory, the glory as of the only begotten of the Father,) full of grace and truth."

A careful reading of this chapter makes it clear that Jesus Christ is in view. But this is not the only place in the Scriptures where He is identified as the Word. This name was used by the Apostle John in his description of our Lord in His Second-Coming glory: "And he was clothed with a vesture dipped in blood: and his name is called The Word of God" (Rev. 19:13). Consequently, then, we can say from these Scriptures that one of the names of the Lord Jesus Christ is "the Word of God."

Paul testified to the truth of the Incarnation, Christ's coming in the flesh, when he wrote: "God was manifest in the flesh, justified in the Spirit, seen of angels, preached unto the Gentiles, believed on in the world, received up into glory" (I Tim. 3:16). Could anything be plainer? Christ was God, and He was made visible to men by coming in the form of a man.

In His high-priestly prayer, recorded in John 17, our Lord addressed the Father in these words: "O Father, glorify thou me with thine own self with the glory which I had with thee before the world was" (v. 5). Jesus asserted His eternal existence.

The Old Testament is not silent on this matter either. We read in Micah 5:2: "But thou, Bethlehem Ephratah, though thou be little among the thousands of Judah, yet out of thee shall he come forth unto me that is to be ruler in Israel; whose goings forth have been from of old, from everlasting." According to this verse, Jesus Christ has always existed.

Isaiah presented the same truth in a very unusual way. He said, "For unto us a child is born, unto us a son is given" (Isa. 9:6). Is there any difference between the birth of a child and the giving of a son? There is a vast difference! Jesus was the virgin-born son of Mary, and at the same time He was the eternal Son of God, given for the salvation of mankind.

Had Jesus been merely a man, even though a perfect man, He could not have died for the sins of mankind. He had to be more than a man, and the Scriptures represent Him as more than a man. He is the God-man. (See also such passages as Heb. 10:5 with Matt. 1:20; Gal. 4:4,5; John 16:27; Phil. 2:5-8).

A Warning

We have seen what our attitude is to be toward those who do not teach or falsely teach the doctrine of Christ, but the subject needs much fuller treatment. John wrote: "If there come any unto you, and bring not this doctrine [that Jesus is eternally God], receive him not into your house, neither bid him God speed: for he that biddeth him

God speed is partaker of his evil deeds" (II John 1:10,11).

We know from the Scriptures that we are to exercise the love of God in our dealings with men and women. We must exercise it in this matter also. But, under these circumstances, we show our love for God by not supporting those who deny the truth. Since they are enemies of the truth, we are not to identify ourselves with them or help their efforts by supporting them in any way. We are to love them as sinners needing a Saviour, but we are not to treat them as servants of God, for they are not. They are imposters.

Some members of God's family today are guilty of supporting such false teachers. These born-again ones may even belong to churches which deny that Christ is the eternal God, that He is a member of the Trinity, that He was virgin born. And their money is given to foster these denials of our Christian faith.

But let me warn again that we must be sure of our facts. This particular passage is used by some today to apply to people who do not agree with them on certain doctrinal matters or on certain methods of evangelism. That is a wrong use of this verse. Be sure you know the facts about those you refuse to support.

Why is this so important? One reason is that some act on the basis of hearsay. We trust what we read or hear about certain individuals and groups. The danger is that if we have not examined the facts for ourselves, we may become guilty of calling someone an imposter who is not an imposter. Watch out for the Devil's cunning devices. He hates the gospel, and he hates the servants of the Lord

Jesus Christ. If he can, he will try to get us to believe that some preachers are imposters when they are not. But when we have the facts and know that certain men deny the virgin birth of Christ and other basic truths, we are not to bid them God-speed. If we do, we join with them in their evil deeds.

Supporting the Brethren

In III John is a very clear statement about those we should support: "Beloved, thou doest faithfully whatsoever thou doest to the brethren, and to strangers; which have borne witness of thy charity [love] before the church: whom if thou bring forward on their journey after a godly sort, thou shalt do well: because that for his name's sake they went forth, taking nothing of the Gentiles. We therefore ought to receive such, that we might be fellow-helpers to the truth" (vv. 5-8).

The only marks of identification given concerning those whom John called brethren are "for his name's sake they went forth" (v. 7).

That they were not the religious leaders of Christ's day is very clear from what our Saviour said, as He addressed the scribes and Pharisees. They were the religious leaders of that time, but they did not represent the average believer who trusted in Christ. Our Saviour said to them, "Search the scriptures; for in them ye think ye have eternal life: and they are they which testify of me" (John 5:39). He was saying, in effect, "You think you have eternal life on the basis of the Scriptures. Why don't you search them? The same Scriptures that seem to tell you that you have eternal life are the very Scriptures that testify concerning me."

And then He added these words: "And ye will not come to me, that ye might have life. I receive not honour from men. But I know you, that ye have not the love of God in you. I am come in my Father's name, and ye receive me not: if another shall come in his own name, him ye will receive. How can ye believe, which receive honour one of another, and seek not the honour that cometh from God only?" (vv. 40-44).

The brethren of whom John spoke in III John are the very opposite of these religious leaders. They went out in the name of Jesus Christ and truly believed in His virgin birth. They believed that He walked on the earth and was the eternal Christ, the eternal God, the Creator of the universe and the Saviour of the world. This they believed, and because they were born of God they went out in the name of Jesus, proclaiming His truth. John said the Christians were to send forward and to support such men as these.

John did not say that it was necessary for the Christians to agree with these men in every detail of doctrine. But because these men taught the basic truths of the Word, they were to be helped on their way by God's people.

It is sad to see how our sense of values has changed since those New Testament days. There is so much contention at the present time between various groups of Christians. Some take the position that they will not support anyone except those in their own denomination and fellowship. God is calling forth His servants today, as in every day, and is telling His people to support them since they go forward in the name of Jesus Christ. Some of them may not belong to our denomination. They may even be willing to work on an interdenominational basis so that they can reach more for Christ. But because they do, some of us close our doors to them.

Some pastors refuse to support missionaries who work under fundamental, Bible-believing mission boards, and they close their churches to them, even though they believe and teach the truth. Such people will have to reckon with God. His work must go on. We are to support those who go forth in the name of Jesus Christ, and we will have to reckon with God at the Judgment Seat of Christ if we go contrary to His program.

We have had letters from heartbroken Christians who have passed through this very experience. Through the Back to the Bible Broadcast or other avenues of ministry, they had come to realize the need for stepping out of churches where modernists controlled the church program and where the truth of the gospel was denied.

Then, after leaving Modernism, they joined a Bible-believing church only to be told that the church supported only the Christian work of its own denomination. All gifts had to be channeled through their church treasurer to the works endorsed by the official board. Any members of the congregation who wanted to support other phases of Christian work had to leave the church.

Domineering Diotrephes

Third John also warns believers to beware of and avoid people who spread evil and unfounded reports about God's servants. We need to examine our own hearts to make sure that these next verses do not describe us. They do not describe false teachers but those who are fundamental in their faith. They believe the truth concerning God and Christ and the virgin birth, and yet they harm the cause of Christ.

"I wrote unto the church," said John, "but Diotrephes, who loveth to have the preeminence among them, receiveth us not. Wherefore, if I come, I will remember his deeds which he doeth, prating against us with malicious words: and not content therewith, neither doth he himself receive the brethren, and forbiddeth them that would, and casteth them out of the church. Beloved, follow not that which is evil, but that which is good. He that doeth good is of God: but he that doeth evil hath not seen God" (vv. 9-11).

This is a serious indictment which God sets forth against those who, for personal and selfish reasons, refuse to support certain servants of Christ and cast out of the church those who insist on meeting their God-given obligations. This very thing is going on in Christian circles today. This is to our shame.

Let us examine ourselves in the light of His Word and see where we really stand with reference to these things. May God help all of us to see and to meet our responsibilities and, above all, to be true to Him who loved us and washed us from our sins in His own blood.